Mez McConnell's abusive childhood left him mostly dead, but God's grace revived him. This book tells that sensational story and offers hope, because what happened to Mez can happen to others. *The Creaking on the Stairs* is especially important because the hero of the book is not Mez or some nice person or the social gospel: It's *doctrine*, including God's sovereignty and Christ's atonement. Church leaders with academic backgrounds can learn from Mez not to dumb down theology when preaching to poor congregations. Those who have hit bottom need not soothing words but the hard Gospel truths of sin and deliverance.

MARVIN OLASKY
Editor in chief, *World*

By writing, *The Creaking On The Stairs* Mez McConnell has provided a gift to the Church. The beauty of the book is that Mez tells the story of his own suffering and folds it into the bigger story of the gospel of Jesus Christ. It is heartbreaking, empathetic, accessible, and pastorally wise. Moreover, it presents the reader with the sovereign, holy and merciful God of the Bible who alone can bring lasting light and hope into darkness and despair. Anyone can read this. Everyone should.

GAVIN PEACOCK
Associate Pastor, Calvary Grace Church of Calgary
Director of International Outreach for CBMW
co- author of *The Grand Design: Male And Female He Made Them*

Mez writes with courage and compassion. The courage to tell his painful story. And compassion to point us to the place of healing. Read the book and expect to be shocked by depravity and deliverance.

ERIK RAYMOND
Senior Pastor, Redeemer Fellowship Church, Boston, Massachusetts
Author of *Chasing Contentment, Gospel Shaped Outreach,* and *Is Hell for Real?*

Few things are more horrific than for a child to be tortured by someone who was supposed to love them. Scars of abuse go deeper than burn marks or lashes can leave. Somehow abuse scars the soul and tempts the heart to never risk letting people get close. Yet, in *The Creaking on the Stairs*, Mez bravely invites you into his painful past and gives hope through the grace of Jesus who entered into our pain-riddled world. Whether you are a believer in God or not, whether you have suffered abuse or not, I cannot more highly commend this work to you.

J. GARRETT KELL

Pastor, Del Ray Baptist Church, Alexandria, Virginia

Can victims of abuse find wholeness through the gospel of Christ? Are faith and forgiveness sufficient remedies for the soul-damage abusers inflict? Scripture says 'yes', emphatically. But as countless believers know, the wounds of abuse aren't always healed instantly or automatically. In fact, those hurts are used by God in the testing of our faith that produces steadfastness (James 1:3). The injuries of our past thus become the instruments of our sanctification.

Mez McConnell explores this truth in a deeply personal, gut-wrenchingly candid account of his own struggle with bitter emotions and smouldering resentment. Writing with unvarnished honesty, he describes the conflict between righteous anger and forgiveness—and he points the way to liberty and triumph in the grace of God. If you're seeking help for yourself or for others in the aftermath of abuse, this book is a wonderful resource. And no matter who you are or where you have come from, Mez will motivate you to love Christ and hate sin more than ever.

PHIL JOHNSON

Executive Director of *Grace to You*
Pastor, Grace Community Church, Sun Valley, California

It's been said that we're all 'soaked with the sense of exile' and long for restored Eden. The hope for the abused and the abuser alike is in Jesus Christ who is indeed making all things new (Rev. 21:5). Born of unimaginable pain, this book will surely be a gospel balm to many.

CHRIS LARSON
President & CEO, Ligonier Ministries

I really did not enjoy this book... but I am thankful for it. And I am convinced that it is vital reading for us. Mez points to the power of a loving, suffering Lord to save and heal even from the most harrowing abuse. Whether you've suffered abuse or grew up safe and loved, read it. It is an invaluable resource as we serve the abused and suffering in our midst with the love of Jesus. Simultaneously, gruelling and glorious.

STEVE TIMMIS
Director of Acts29

Raw. Real. Redemptive. The story of Mez McConnell's childhood abuse, interestingly, neither centres on himself or his tormentors, but rather on God's good and sovereign providence, and a suffering Saviour who gave himself for Mez, and all who trust in him. It could have been just crushing, but instead it is filled with hope. Mez could have been trapped in a vortex of bitterness and recrimination, but was set free by his Redeemer to a life of forgiveness and fullness. If you have experienced abuse that has led you away from Jesus, the church and the Gospel, Mez will show you the way back home. I'm deeply thankful for Mez, a trophy of Grace and a faithful shepherd.

LIGON DUNCAN
Chancellor and CEO, Reformed Theological Seminary

Painfully raw and profoundly helpful, this is a book that speaks into the depths of our darkness and offers extraordinary hope for both the abused and the abusers. If you feel ashamed, hopeless and bitter - or you know someone who does - you must read this.

MIKE REEVES

President & Professor of Theology, Union School of Theology, Wales

With vivid personal stories, well-stated research, and a storehouse of scripture, Mez takes the grievous and gut-wrenching reality of abuse and holds it up to the light of grace. While I wish this book didn't have to exist, I'm thankful it does. It's a powerful and redemptive resource.

EMILY JENSEN

Cofounder of Risen Motherhood

Co-author of *Risen Motherhood: Gospel Hope for Everyday Moments*

If the 'problem of evil' exists in your mind as an abstract theoretical issue, this book will help you come face to face with it in a personal way. These stories will haunt you. If you have endured childhood abuse, Mez's terror-filled memories may uncover a pain deep within your own soul. Don't let that be a deterrent, take heart. Rather than leave you in the cold darkness of his experiences or your own memories, Mez points you to the warming light of the world. In this book, you will be drawn to the present comfort and promised hope of Jesus Christ. And, even if every question is not answered, you will finish this book knowing these things for sure: You are not alone, God loves you intimately, and Jesus will make all things new. The two-fold testimony of Mez's vulnerability and Christ's sufficiency will certainly aid in bringing healing to the broken.

MATTHEW Z. CAPPS

Senior Pastor, Fairview Baptist Church, Apex, North Carolina

Beaten with fists and broomsticks. Imprisoned, starved, and neglected. Physically, sexually, and emotionally abused. From a life of drugs, violence, and hatred to one of pastoring, church planting, and advocacy. With honesty and grace, Mez McConnell weaves together the scope of his abuse and recovery with the scope of Jesus' person and work. In short, accessible chapters he outlines the hope of the Gospel available to both survivors and abusers. Highly recommended.

ERIC SCHUMACHER

Shepherd, Songwriter, Storyteller at emschumacher.com
Co-author with Elyse Fitzpatrick of *Worthy: Celebrating the Value of Women* (forthcoming)

Mez McConnell is bold and brash, he is a powerful preacher and he leads an exciting work among the under-served peoples in the hard places of our cities and communities. He is theologically astute, and one would be well advised not to underestimate his wisdom. He is also brutally honest – honest about his own past and honest about his present nightmares. That he has become the man he is today is a tribute to the grace of God at work in him. This book not only tells his story, it gives us clear strategies for identifying abuse when it happens and what steps to take to intervene. All of us will learn from the deep life lessons found here. I am profoundly grateful to know him and for his courage to speak out. To God be the glory.

LIAM GOLIGHER

Author, Bible teacher, and conference speaker
Senior Minister of Tenth Presbyterian Church, Philadelphia, Pennsylvania

Both within the church and without, more and more people are talking about their experiences with childhood abuse. Whether we are the ones who have suffered abuse or whether we are attempting to walk alongside friends or family members, *The Creaking On The Stairs* will prove a helpful resource. I finished it with the sober but thankful realisation that in its pages Mez has given us something incredibly valuable: truth and hope. He has given us truth that can be applied to even the most broken situations, and hope for that day when there will be no more weeping and no more tears. For that reason and many more, I can't recommend this book enough.

AILEEN CHALLIES
Pastor's Wife

Reading about the reality of child abuse in the life of someone you know is gut wrenching. Realising the prevalence of abuse in our world is overwhelmingly distressing. Mez's personal account of his life is a hard read, but as the grace and mercy of God is put on display in his life, it proves also to be a hopeful read. On the bleak and dark canvas of abuse, the gospel can shine. It shines brightly on these pages as Mez wonderfully notes hope for the abused and the abuser, as well as for ministers seeking to shepherd both.

ANTHONY MATHENIA
Pastor, Christchurch, Radford, Virginia

This book is heart-wrenching but necessary. It applies the gospel in the worst of contexts and demonstrates its power to save and restore. It is written for those who are hurting and for those who long to minister to them. These pages are void of whitewash, trite answers and cliché, but full of the gospel!

PAUL WASHER
President, Heart Cry Ministry, Radford, Virginia

Mez McConnell has one of the most powerful testimonies I've ever heard. And he's never gotten over the Author's grace. In this searching and timely memoir, my friend recounts the horror of being abused as a child, the painful repercussions ever since, and the unexpected hope he's found. *The Creaking On The Stairs* is a relentlessly evangelistic book. If you struggle to imagine a good God due to past abuse, Mez wants you to know you are not alone. You are not forgotten. You are deeply loved. He can testify to that firsthand.

MATT SMETHURST

Managing editor of The Gospel Coalition
and author of *Before You Open Your Bible: Nine Heart Postures for Approaching God's Word*

The Creaking On The Stairs will reach out and grasp your soul. Your heart will be provoked in a multiplicity of directions and draw out of you a depth of emotions. For those who have been acquainted with abuse, a new song of freedom and healing will resonate as you hear the message of Jesus' work on the cross. Mez has carefully crafted a theologically rich, pastorally gentle, Christ-exalting tool. This is much needed in Christ's global church. Get it, read it, teach it, and heed it.

DOUG LOGAN

Director of the Diversity Initiative, Acts 29
Co-director of Church in Hard Places

The book you hold in your hands is unlike anything I have ever read. Mez McConnell shares his story of the horrific child abuse he endured with a raw and honest transparency that made me weep through most of the book. But he doesn't stop there. He weaves a rich, biblical theology and gospel clarity throughout it in such a moving manner that brings the truth of God's steadfast love for sinners unmistakably alive. Never have I experienced a book that is for the abused and abuser; the victimised and the tormentor. And the power of the gospel being the answer for all. Stunningly accessible and beautifully written, this book is sure to be a healing balm to the soul of many abuse survivors and a defining book for a generation.

BRIAN CROFT

Senior Pastor, Auburndale Baptist Church,
Founder, Practical Shepherding
Senior Fellow, Revitalization Center,
Southern Baptist Theological Seminary, Louville, Kentucky

Gripping from the very first page, Mez McConnell's *The Creaking On The Stairs* is a painfully raw, sweetly pastoral, and deeply theological word to those who have suffered abuse. Mez's own heart-breaking story pulses through these pages, but even that pales in comparison to the good news that Jesus – though He himself suffered abuse, rejection, and shame – now offers love and compassion to broken, sinful people. This is a book that will speak to the hearts of many, and that will also open the hearts of many to understand the ravages of abuse and the healing power of the Saviour. You don't just read this book; you experience it.

GREG GILBERT

Senior Pastor, Third Avenue Baptist Church, Louisville, Kentucky

THE
CREAKING
ON THE
STAIRS

FINDING FAITH IN GOD
THROUGH CHILDHOOD ABUSE

MEZ M^cCONNELL

Copyright © Mez McConnell 2019

paperback ISBN 978-1-5271-0441-9
epub ISBN 978-1-5271-0496-9
mobi ISBN 978-1-5271-0497-6

10 9 8 7 6 5 4 3 2 1

Published in 2019
by
Christian Focus Publications Ltd,
Geanies House, Fearn, Ross-shire,
IV20 1TW, Great Britain.

www.christianfocus.com

Cover and interior design by MOOSE77

Printed and bound
by Bell & Bain, Glasgow

CONTENTS

This book is dedicated to Jesus Christ, my Lord & Saviour.

My wife, Miriam, who has shared my life for the past 25 years.

My daughters, Keziah & Lydia, because they wanted to see their names in this book. Well, here they are!

My fellow elders & church members, for allowing me the time off to write this thing.

Matthew Spandler Davison, my Co-Director of 20schemes, international travel companion, champion of Acts 29 Church In Hard Places, fellow abuse sufferer & friend.

A special mention to Katie Johnson, my favourite-ever person, who worked long and hard on the design and edits with me.

FOREWORD

This is the most disturbing book that I have ever read, and I cannot recommend it highly enough.

This book will offend and challenge and upset you in all the right ways.

After reading this book, you will shudder at the thought of using the gospel as a pep talk or a clean-up job. And you will cover your mouth with your hand and repent of every time you have done this.

This book is unusual and vital and risky.

It will expose the polite fakery of our cleaned-up evangelicalism.

But like all good books, this book isn't about you or me.

It is about the resurrected Jesus Christ and the unimaginable suffering of millions of abused children who cry out to a God that they have never met, only to be left in deafening silence.

This book unmasks the questions we rarely dare to whisper: If God is so loving, why does He allow innocent children to suffer horrific abuse by the hands of their parents? If God is so sovereign, why does He allow parents to neglect and abandon their children? If God loves you and has a perfect plan for your life, then why do teenagers kill one another? If God won't give you more than you can handle, then why do people kill themselves?

Mez's answer to these questions did not come easily. He bears the marks on his body and mind. He knows the secret shame. The adults who silently observed his hell and torment and cast their gaze away are frozen in a mirror of memories. He still hears the cries of his sister. And the rage and anger from never having the chance to defend himself or his sister from his tormentor consumed him for decades. Mez tried to stop the dam of these monstrous memories with all of the things he could control: drugs and knives and grit and women.

And then Jesus, in the form of a prison sentence, broke into his world. The resurrected Christ who knows no barriers and respects no persons came to Mez in prison, working through ordinary Christians. They compelled Mez to do one simple and dangerous thing: 'Consider him, who endured from sinners such hostility against himself, so that you may not grow weary and faint-hearted' **(Hebrews 12:3)**. But they did not come at once. And they did not come only with words. They came often and with a house key and an invitation to live with them upon his release.

Consider Jesus. Mez's first response was to defend himself against such hard-hearted counsel. His years in foster care assembled social worker after social worker who told him that his problems were his parents, his abusive childhood, the starvation and the violation and the diabolic infamy of the words of the stepmother whose voice only got louder in his mind after she left. These well-intended social workers preached the gospel of social justice: People are born good, but their environment and the adults around them make them bad. Mez—like all of us—

had to choose. We simply can't believe that our environment is both problem and solution and 'consider Jesus' at the same time.

The story of the resurrected Christ is not for the faint of heart. And this book's author, resurrected by Christ, bears scars from a lifetime of childhood abuse. But what happens to those scars when they are covered by the blood of Christ? That answer is the jewel of this book.

This is a book written for multiple audiences. One, the most precious one, are the adult survivors of childhood abuse. The men and women and children whose lives are shipwrecked and who are living in a shell of pain and unanswered questions. Mez talks directly to abuse survivors on the pages that you hold in your hand. He articulates the questions that haunt and hurt and slowly teases out the grace of listening and the gospel that does not move quickly to answers. Gospel grace holds suffering and sufferers dear, and the answers that come from grace are neither easy nor safe nor quick. There is so much potential healing on the pages of this book. Mez has blazed a trail of tears for others to follow to the foot of the Cross.

The other audience Mez graciously includes on these pages are believers who want to help but who know that easy answers end up as hollow daggers in someone's heart. As we read this pastoral tome, we watch Mez build a bridge from the abuse survivor, who hurts all over, to Jesus, the only One who understands the depth of this hurt. The bridge that Mez builds does not reduce its theology to anemic blather about worldview or apologetic bombs. Christian, your worldview and your apologetics will not help a soul without the compassion and the victory of the resurrected Christ. In putting the hand of the sufferer into the hand of the Savior, Mez reveals how a reformed understanding of sin and grace allows the survivor of abuse to ask and answer the hardest of all questions: *why?*

Indeed.

This is the most disturbing book that I have ever read. And I cannot recommend it highly enough.

Rosaria Butterfield
Durham, North Carolina, 2019
Author of *The Secret Thoughts of an Unlikely Convert* (2012), *Openness Unhindered* (2015), and *The Gospel Comes with a House Key* (2018).

AUTHOR'S NOTE

In 1987, my father married a wonderful woman, Maureen, who was nothing but loving and kind to me (and my sister). They have remained married for the past 32 years and have been extremely happy together. In no way do the events described in this book reflect on her. Also, my father never raised a hand against me in my life and is, for the most part, completely unaware of many of the events I describe in the pages of this book. The abuse I talk about within this book happened to me between the ages of two and thirteen, long before my father met and married Maureen.

The only person who could truly understand what happened during those early years would be my sister, Tracy, although we were sometimes separated. Indeed, I am sure she has her own memories of events and her own experiences could fill a book all on its own.

We have never really talked about what happened to us as children, but I can tell you that she was a great big sister and stood up for me, often at a painful cost to herself.

I am also extremely proud of the life she has gone on to make for herself, despite the trauma of our early childhood.

INTRODUCTION

A couple of years ago, I was lying in bed when a message popped up on social media. A name flashed across the screen. The name of the woman who had been my tormentor for most of my early childhood.

She had died.

I could scarcely believe it. All the old feelings, dormant for nearly three decades, rose to the surface. Anger, guilt and shame. They all came calling that night. And so I did what I always do when trying to process my emotions.

I wrote.

I wrote a blog in the early hours of the morning and posted it, hoping that it would be helpful to some. Forty-eight hours and half a million hits later, I realised that I was not alone in my secret shame. There was a world of childhood pain and suffering out there in the church.

And if this is true for God's people, then I can only imagine the extent of the torment and suffering for millions outside of the church of Jesus Christ.

Here's what I wrote that night…

DING DONG THE WICKED WITCH IS DEAD!

In a recent obituary, some of the children of a newly deceased mother wrote this startling piece for their local press. This is not my stepmother's obituary, but it definitely could be.

> *Marianne Theresa Johnson-Reddick born Jan 4, 1935 and died alone on Sept. 30, 2013. She is survived by 6 of her 8 children whom she spent her lifetime torturing in every way possible. While she neglected and abused her small children, she refused to allow anyone else to care or show compassion towards them. When they became adults, she stalked and tortured anyone they dared to love. Everyone she met, adult or child, was tortured by her cruelty and exposure to violence, criminal activity, vulgarity, and hatred of the gentle or kind human spirit.*
>
> *On behalf of her children whom she so abrasively exposed to her evil and violent life, we celebrate her passing from this earth and hope she lives in the afterlife reliving each gesture of violence, cruelty and shame that she delivered on her children. Her surviving children will now live the rest of their lives with the peace of knowing their nightmare finally has some form of closure.[1]*

---

1   A report on the obituary can be found here: https://www.snopes.com/fact-check/death-penalty/

I just heard several hours ago that my stepmother of almost 13 years is dead. Of what and how I do not know. **She** was young. I know that. So painful is it even to think of her name I refer to her as **'she'** throughout my autobiography.[2]

> It's 1:30am and I can't sleep. I don't know what to think or to feel.

The words above are pretty much what I would like to express to the world. I would like to go to her funeral, stand and let everybody know what this person was truly like and how much damage **she** did while alive. I want her to get her just desserts even though I know, thanks to Christ, I will never get my own.

> I am a pastor. I should know better. I do know better.

I know, deep in my soul, that Jesus experienced every form of suffering when He was in the world. *'He was despised and rejected by men; a man of sorrows, and acquainted with grief'* **(Isaiah 53:3)**. Jesus was betrayed and tortured. He is well acquainted with my grief, and I know that the Bible teaches that He will never leave me **(John 14:18)**. I know, therefore, that perceived wisdom (my own included) demands that I forgive this woman who caused me so much pain as a child. I know it's the Christian thing to do. I know, according to what the Bible teaches, that *he who has been forgiven much ought to forgive much in return.*

> I know. I really do.

> And yet...

---

2   McConnell, M *Is There Anybody Out There? A Journey From Despair To Hope* (Ross-Shire: CFP, 2011).

...I want to make public my frustration at crimes **she** never paid for. I want to scream it out loud for all to hear.

And yet...

...I want to be magnanimous in my forgiveness to her as Christ has been to me in forgiving my sin.

I just feel so conflicted.

I thought I might dance a little jig or at least feel a sense of release and elation at news I'd dreamed about and ached for as a child. This was a woman who drove me to such despair that I attempted to set her on fire in her (drunken) sleep when I was no more than 10 years old.

But there is no jig. There is no elation. There is no sense of release.

There is just a heaviness of heart and the nagging itch of my suffering and her evil never admitted in this life. The problem is that I want to feel joy at her passing. I want to rejoice in the belief that **she** will face the judge of all the earth for her crimes against me. I want to revel in the thought that **she** is having her own spiritual Nuremburg moment before Almighty God right now. That Father Time has caught up with her, and her sins are about to be found out and brought into that terrible, perfect light. That the angels in glory will see just what a monster **she** truly was.

But I just don't feel the joy that I want to. Instead, I feel sad. Sad for a woman who wasted her life in bitter anger and expressed it through the mental and physical torture of children. Sad for the trail of devastation **she** left behind. Sad for the family members **she** hurt and betrayed. Sad that, despite these things, people will mourn her passing. There will be tears at her funeral.

There will be stories of her good side or of things well done and said. Things I never experienced. Things I can scarcely believe are true about her.

I am conflicted even further when I think about my own family today, almost three decades after **she** beat me for the last time. My wife of 20 years lies next to me soundly sleeping. My teenage girls are in their rooms. Because of the scars of my childhood, they have never known violence in our home. Because of the horrors of my pain, they have never known cigarette burns on pale, skinny arms. Because of the nightmare of systematic abuse I faced, they have never spent endless lonely nights in locked cupboards without food and clothing. Because of my shame, they have never known the horrors of being stripped and mocked in front of drunken strangers. Because of my humiliations, they have never known hunger so deep they've been forced to eat their own faeces. Because of the extreme violence of my upbringing, they've never been beaten with poles and sticks. Because of the trauma of my childhood, they've never been knocked unconscious for failing to wash a dish properly.

Ironically, because of 'her', my own children have never known the horrors of deeply psychological and traumatic abuse.

Of course, there is another reason they have never known and experienced these things. They've never known these things because I know Jesus. I know the bittersweet truth of Genesis in my own life. 'As for you, you meant evil against me, but God meant it for good, to bring it about that many people should be kept alive, as they are today' **(Genesis 50:20 ESV)**.

I am conflicted because I realise that my own family lie peaceably unmolested because of God's goodness in my life and, perversely, her evil in it too. God has used her evil for good. The thought that my pain has been used for good comforts me as I grapple with why these things were permitted to happen to me. The thought that **she** should get any credit is abhorrent.

Even now, at 2:30am as I trawl through online press cuttings and see familiar faces all over the court's pages and the obituaries, I feel a deep gratitude for Jesus. Old family and friends imprisoned and/or dead at criminally young ages. And I find her photo. **She** looks like an old woman even though **she** was not. A lifetime of self-abuse has ravaged her features.

That could have been me. That was my own road to self-destruction until Jesus intervened. I live today only because Jesus found me and turned my life around. He gave me hope. He gave me a spiritual family. Brothers and sisters who have loved and cared for me. He used godly people to teach me personal responsibility for my own sins. He used godly people to teach me how to be a real man, a faithful husband, a loving father and an (average) pastor.

He is teaching me still.

Yet, still I feel conflicted. I am angry with myself. I feel like my to-ing and fro-ing over forgiveness and the rationalisation of my suffering is somehow betraying my childhood self. A spiritual battle rages on. The old man berates the new while the latter fights for peace. The old man wants to take me on a trip down (painful) memory lane, trawling up old wounds and savage rage long since soothed with the balm of the gospel. Of course, he's popped by from time to time in my Christian life, but it seems like he's pulled an armchair up tonight and he's here for an extended visit.

The new man is winning.

Just.

Two decades of living for Jesus have evened the odds against two decades of self-loathing, shame, anger and destruction. It seems that even the sovereign control over her death means that I am able to be conflicted without complete self-implosion. The same Holy Spirit that raised Christ from the dead is helping me to draw on my decades of biblical knowledge and personal experience with which to vanquish the poisonous darts of the devil.

It's 4am and I am suddenly reminded that I am not the person I was 30 years ago. Maybe **she** did change at the end? An awful thought crosses my mind. What if **she**, like me, found the true forgiveness and peace of Jesus Christ? No. There was no evidence to suggest it. How would I know? I haven't seen her for 30 years. No! Surely not? God wouldn't do that to me? He's on my side, right? He wouldn't let me down by saving my chief tormentor, would He?

Imagine that.

That would be the ultimate cheat, wouldn't it? Pardoned, at the death, for her heinous crimes against me and who knows how many others? I don't like that thought.

I realise that, if it were true, then I'd be like the angry brother in the Parable of the Prodigal.

I want God to overlook my sins. I like it when He does that. But hers? That's a stretch. I tell myself I'm a better person than **she** was. Is that true? Maybe now. But any good in me belongs to the Holy Spirit. I hurt people. I abused people. I stole. I lied. I murdered in my heart. I too have done awful things.

I think about **Romans 12:17-21**:

Do not repay anyone evil for evil. Be careful to do what is right in the eyes of everyone. If it is possible, as far as it depends on you, live at peace with everyone. Do not take revenge, my friends, but leave room for God's wrath, for it is written: 'It is mine to avenge; I will repay,' says the Lord. On the contrary: If your enemy is hungry, feed him; if he is thirsty, give him something to drink. In doing this, you will heap burning coals on his head.' Do not be overcome by evil, but overcome evil with good.

I don't like that very much. I want to be her judge and jury.

Do I trust God to be hard enough on her? Will He let her off on a technicality? Will He forgive her? Maybe He doesn't know the full story, and I need to fill him in on the details.

Pathetic, I know.

Sinful.

Arrogant.

I want to comfort myself by comparing my innocent suffering to his. Jesus understands me because we have suffered together. But, tragic though it is, it doesn't really compare to His cosmic distress. My pain, though real, is not even a pinprick on the little finger of His nail-pierced hand. My suffering is infinitesimal in light of the cross of Calvary. He died for awful human beings like my stepmother.

Like me.

I roll over and try to sleep, chewing on that awful truth.

She doesn't need my forgiveness any more than I need her repentance. We both need the former from Him, and He requires the latter from us.

Thankfully, in Jesus He grants both to all who come.

It doesn't tie it all up in a neat little bow, but at least sleep comes knowing that, ultimately, the judge of all the earth will do right and act justly.

THIS BOOK IS FOR THE SILENT SUFFERERS WITHIN OUR CHURCHES (AND WITHOUT)

It is for the hundreds around the world who emailed me their own stories of painful abuse and trauma. It is for those who have hidden their guilty secrets, too scared to speak out. It is for those whose lives have spiralled into self-destructive chaos as they have been unable to process their emotions in adulthood. It is for the scared children cowering under tables and in cupboards as violence and terror surround them. It is for the untold victims struggling to find meaning, hope, and peace out of the wreckage of their lives. It is for the Christian wondering if God truly does love them. It is for the skeptic and the unbeliever who wonders if God exists and, if He does, why He would allow such things to happen. It's for the perpetrators of such vile acts who wonder if their dark deeds will ever be discovered. It's for the ones who've turned their backs on their evil sins and found the cure of forgiveness and peace in Jesus. And it's for the ones who are just not there yet; who wonder if they can ever forgive. Or if they can ever love. If they can ever rebuild their lives. This is a book for all of us.

Abused and abusers. The innocents and the monsters.

HOWEVER, THIS BOOK WON'T ANSWER ALL YOUR QUESTIONS

What book could ever do that? It won't eradicate your pain. It won't take away the nightmares. But, I hope that it will light a pathway to peace with God and release for your soul. I pray that it will open a window on the difficult path travelled by a fellow sufferer in the hope that you too, even though you may not believe it now, may find love, peace and even a measure of healing in the arms of Jesus Christ.

WHAT DO WE MEAN BY 'CHILDHOOD ABUSE'?

We can't begin to get to grips with a topic like this unless we work on a few definitions. Here's what I know for certain as I write this book. *I am not going to be able to cover every single type of abuse*. Let me make that clear from the start. It just isn't possible, let alone feasible. So, let me set some parameters and, hopefully, we can work forward from there.

The World Health Organisation (WHO) defines **child abuse** and **child maltreatment** as *'all forms of physical and/or emotional ill-treatment, sexual abuse, neglect or negligent treatment or commercial or other exploitation, resulting in actual or potential harm to the child's health, survival, development or dignity in the context of a relationship of responsibility, trust or power.'*[1]

J. D. Vance, in his memoir, *Hillbilly Elegy*[2], refers to the *Adverse Childhood Experiences*[3] test as a barometer for gauging the

---

1   'Child abuse and neglect by parents and other caregivers' (PDF). World Health Organisation. Chapter 3.
2   *Hillbilly Elegy: A Memoir of a Family and Culture in Crisis* (NY: HarperCollins, 2016)
3   https://www.cdc.gov/violenceprevention/acestudy/

acuteness (or otherwise) of the trauma faced in childhood. When I took the test, I scored 10/10. The aim here is not to enter into a competition about who has had the worst traumatic experiences, but to try and clarify our terms as best we can at the outset of this book.

Because I cannot cover every form of childhood maltreatment and abuse, for the sake of simplicity, I am going to categorise abuse and/or maltreatment as falling into one of the following four categories.

Sexual Abuse
Physical Abuse
Emotional Abuse
Neglect

SEXUAL ABUSE

Again, the definitions here can quickly become complicated and convoluted. But sexual abuse can be both physical and non-physical. The NSPCC calls them **contact abuse** and **non-contact abuse**.[4]

Contact abuse involves touching activities where an abuser makes physical contact with a child, including penetration. It includes:

- sexual touching of any part of the body, whether the child is wearing clothes or not
- rape or penetration by putting an object or body part inside a child's mouth, vagina, or anus
- forcing or encouraging a child to take part in sexual activity

---

4   https://www.nspcc.org.uk/preventing-abuse/child-abuse-and-neglect/child-sexual-abuse/

- making a child take their clothes off, touch someone else's genitals or masturbate.

Non-contact abuse involves non-touching activities, such as grooming, exploitation, persuading children to perform sexual acts over the internet, and flashing. It includes:
- encouraging a child to watch or hear sexual acts
- not taking proper measures to prevent a child being exposed to sexual activities by others
- meeting a child following sexual grooming with the intent of abusing them
- online abuse including making, viewing or distributing child abuse images
- allowing someone else to make, view, or distribute child abuse images
- showing pornography to a child
- sexually exploiting a child for money, power, or status (child exploitation).[5]

PHYSICAL ABUSE

Physical abuse is deliberately hurting a child, causing injuries such as bruises, broken bones, burns or cuts. **It isn't accidental** – children who are physically abused suffer violence such as being hit, kicked, poisoned, burned, slapped, or having objects thrown at them. Shaking or hitting babies can cause non-accidental head injuries. Sometimes parents or carers will make up or cause the symptoms of illness in their child, perhaps giving them medicine

---

5   https://www.nspcc.org.uk/preventing-abuse/child-abuse-and-neglect/child-sexual-abuse/

they don't need and making the child unwell – this is known as fabricated or induced illness.[6]

EMOTIONAL ABUSE

Emotional abuse is the ongoing emotional maltreatment or emotional neglect of a child. It's sometimes called psychological abuse and can seriously damage a child's emotional health and development. Emotional abuse can involve deliberately trying to scare or humiliate a child, or isolating or ignoring them.[7]

NEGLECT

Neglect is the ongoing failure to meet a child's basic needs and is the most common form of child abuse.

- A child may be left hungry or dirty, without adequate clothing, shelter, supervision, medical or health care.
- A child may be put in danger or not protected from physical or emotional harm.
- They may not get the love, care and attention they need from their parents.[8]

In 2011, the NSPCC[9] produced a report of their findings on child abuse in the UK. They discovered the following:

A substantial minority of children experience severe maltreatment and abuse at home, in school and in the community, from adults and from peers.

---

6   https://www.nspcc.org.uk/preventing-abuse/child-abuse-and-neglect/physical-abuse/

7   https://www.nspcc.org.uk/preventing-abuse/child-abuse-and-neglect/emotional-abuse/

8   https://www.nspcc.org.uk/preventing-abuse/child-abuse-and-neglect/neglect/

9   https://www.nspcc.org.uk/globalassets/documents/research-reports/child-abuse-neglect-uk-today-research-report.pdf

- 1 in 5 children have experienced severe maltreatment
- Children abused by parents or carers are almost 3 times more likely to also witness family violence
- 1 in 3 children sexually abused by an adult didn't tell anyone at the time
- All types of abuse and neglect are associated with poorer mental health
- Strong associations were found between maltreatment, sexual abuse, physical violence, and poorer emotional wellbeing, including self-harm and suicidal thoughts.

Some of their key findings included:
- 65.9 per cent of the contact sexual abuse reported by children and young people (0–17s) was perpetrated by other children and young people under the age of 18.[10]
- 24.1 per cent of 18–24s had experienced sexual abuse, including non-contact offences, by an adult or by a peer at some point in childhood.[11]
- Scotland has the second-highest child murder rate in Western Europe.[12]

CONCLUSION

Maybe you've picked up this book because terrible things have happened to you. Maybe somebody bought it for you. Maybe you're looking for answers to some of your questions. *Why did this happen to me? Is it my fault? Is it somebody else's fault? Whose*

---

10   https://www.nspcc.org.uk/globalassets/documents/research-reports/child-abuse-neglect-uk-today-research-report.pdf Page 9.

11   https://www.nspcc.org.uk/globalassets/documents/research-reports/child-abuse-neglect-uk-today-research-report.pdf Page 9.

12   https://www.nspcc.org.uk/globalassets/documents/research-reports/child-abuse-neglect-uk-today-research-report.pdf Page 17.

fault is it? All you know is that you have been abused and it has affected your whole life. You wonder if you will ever be able to forget. You wonder if the memories will fade and the scars will heal. You wonder whether the guilt will stop, and the shame will go away. Then there's the anger, gnawing at you. Eating away at you like a cancer. There's the unexplained rage and frustrations at people around you – especially your loved ones. There's the unspoken fear that maybe you will turn into the person or people who violated you. The fear that you will turn into an abuser keeps you awake at night and stops you from forming close bonds or having children.

Maybe you've had counselling. Maybe you've had none. Maybe your abuser(s) were caught. Maybe they weren't. Maybe you had an apology. Most likely you have not. Nor, sadly, will you ever.

This book cannot answer many of these questions. But I do think it can still help us.

I know that sounds ridiculous to many of you right now. I know it sounds a bit pie-in-the-sky. I know it sounds too good to be true. Like it will never work for you. That you are too damaged. Too broken. Too angry.

Obviously, it's not going to be easy.

In fact, there is a long road ahead of us.

For some, the journey will be longer than for others. Sadly, far too many of us will sink into a deep depression. We will self-harm, we will drink too much, hide in drugs, or move from one disposable relationship to another. I suspect that far too many of us have been on the road to self-loathing and self-destruction for far too long. Maybe you've grown tired of it. Maybe you've grown tired of life. Tired of waiting for answers that never come. Tired of crying in dark corners.

And now you've found this book. A book about God, you're thinking. What good is this going to do? Let me be up-front with you straight away before we continue.

I think there is real hope to be found, in the middle of our deepest traumas, in the good news about Jesus Christ.

I really do. Don't worry if you don't quite understand that right now. Just hang in with me. Give it a chance before you toss the book to one side. After all, what harm can it do?

I also think that there is a place for us to find hope and community within the church.

Because of these two beliefs, I truly think, distant though it may be, that *we may even get to a place of peace within our souls and a place of forgiveness for those who hurt us so much.*

Read that last sentence again.

No, you didn't read it incorrectly.

Yes, I know that it sounds outrageous.

It's probably making you mad even thinking about it. *Forgiving our abusers? No way! That will never happen!* Again, let's hang in and see where this book takes us. What do we have to lose? It's not like we can be in any more pain than we already are, is it?

Most of us, if we even think about God (and I believe most of us do in our quiet moments), have a huge problem with Him. If He even exists then He has a lot of explaining to do, right? *Where was He when all this was going on in our lives? Where was this so-called all-powerful and all-loving God when we were being abused and terrorised? Where was He then, and where is He now?*

There's nothing wrong with these questions. They're perfectly natural. I have asked them myself many, many times over the years. But, stick with it, because I think there may be answers for us within the pages of this book. We may not like some of them, but I offer them nonetheless.

In fact, it is because of the answers found within this book that I was freed from my own life of pain, self-loathing, anger, and bitterness.

As I try to answer your questions, I hope you, too, find the peace you're looking for in the person of Jesus Christ.

But, as I've said, baby steps. Let's start slowly and work our way forward.

THE GOD WHO IS SILENT

I cry to you for help and you do not answer me;
I stand, and you only look at me.

(Job 30:20)

I remember walking home from school with the envelope in my hand. I held it so tight because I thought it would fly away in the wind. There was nothing more important to me in the world. I was fearful and excited at the same time. Excited because the news within could set the mood in the house. Fearful that if it was bad news then I would be in for a world of pain that night.

I slowed my pace as I walked through the alleyway that would open up onto the street where my house was. I passed a church and thought about God. 'God, please let me pass.' I prayed. I wasn't really much of a pray-er and I didn't go to church. But I believed in God. At least I think I did. 'Please let me pass and please let her be in a good mood tonight, God.' I stopped in the street and scrunched my eyes really tight to let God know how serious I was.

I was 11 years old and in my hands were my 11+ exam results. They would determine what High School I would go to. Would it be a comprehensive like the other kids in my neighbourhood, or would it be a Grammar School like the smart kids? I wasn't sure. I wanted to go to the smart school just to annoy my stepmother. **She** was always calling me stupid and thick. **She** told me daily that I would never amount to anything in my life. I was an idiot, like my dad, **she** said. Well, screamed really. **She** screamed a lot. Well, today I had the proof. Was I an idiot or not?

I opened the front door and pushed into the living room. As usual, there was a crowd of people there, drinking, smoking and talking loudly over one another. My dad was at work. I walked nervously over to her chair and handed the envelope over. 'What's this?' **she** spat at me. 'My exam results,' I stammered. **She** ripped the envelope from my fingers and fixed me with a withering scowl. I took a slight step back, experience teaching me to not keep completely out of striking distance, which would only anger her further, but to be just far enough away for it only to sting when **she** hit out. **She** ripped open the envelope and with it tore a part of the paper within. Her eyes scanned the news and I stood there sweating, praying desperately for a good result and a pain-free evening. 'Please God, please God, please God.' After a couple of moments, **she** crumpled the letter into a ball and threw it at me. 'How did he get on?' one of the strangers asked. 'He passed,' **she** said. The room cheered and soon people were congratulating me and drinking in my honour. **She** just sat there very still. Not looking at me. As if **she** were deep in thought. People were patting me on the head and congratulating me. 'Well done son. Grammar School, eh? I don't know nobody who's went to no Grammar School before.'

Still, **she** was silent. Finally, **she** said to me, 'Go and get yourself a slice of bread for your tea. Put some margarine on it. Not too much though. It's not Christmas.' Wow. Bread and margarine. **She** must be happy with me. 'Thanks, God,' I said inwardly as I went to the kitchen to claim my reward. Two minutes later I was in my room reading the good news for myself. I had passed my exams. I had come within the top 2% in the country. That must mean I wasn't thick (as **she** always told me). I wasn't an idiot after all (**she** said that a lot, too). I smiled to myself and savoured the bread and the creamy margarine. Who knew when I would get a treat like this again?

An hour later I heard the door slamming and the sound of silence descended over the house. Then the sounds of footsteps on the old rotten staircase with the threadbare carpet. My stomach jumped. The all-too-familiar fear came over me. Would **she** pass by and go to bed, or would **she** stumble through the door to my room? A few seconds later I had my answer. My fears realized as the handle turned, the door swung open and **she** stood there, swaying in the doorway, drunk. 'So, you think you're clever, do you?' **she** slurred. 'You think you can show me up in front of my friends?' 'No,' I said. 'Please, God,' I prayed inwardly, earnestly. 'Please, God. Help me. I did my best. I passed. I was a good boy.'

She stormed into the room and aimed a kick at me. I fell off the bed onto the floor and curled into a ball. The kicks kept coming until **she** got tired. Then **she** sat on the edge of the bed and pulled me up by my hair. 'Look at me, you little rat.' **She** spat, 'You're nothing. You'll never be anything. Nobody loves you. Nobody ever will. I don't care what that bit of paper says.' **She** punched me hard, and the darkness came.

That night, something inside me broke. I'm not sure what it was. But I stopped being afraid of her. When I regained consciousness and cleaned myself up, I went to bed happy. I was in pain. But it was a sweet pain. It was the pain of victory. But I was also sad. I had cried out to God. I had cried out to him many times.

But, as usual, there was only silence.

Where was He?
Why had He let this happen to me?
Why didn't He like me?
What had I done to Him?
Did He even care?
Was He even there?

I began to believe that He wasn't.

I JUST DON'T KNOW

There is nothing so cruel in this world as the desolation of having nothing to hope for.
(Haruki Murakami)

I gave up on God when I was very young. It's not like I didn't believe He existed, I just didn't care anymore. He didn't seem relevant to me or my life. In fact, He didn't appear to have made one bit of difference to it. He never stopped the pain or abuse I went through, so what good was He? That was my reasoning and maybe it's yours.

If God exists, then why let children suffer needlessly? Why let me be tortured day after day, year after year, throughout most of my childhood? So, either

(1) God didn't care about me and my pain or
(2) God couldn't do anything about me and my pain or
(3) God didn't exist.

This was the most terrible option for me: The thought that my suffering was pointless, that none of it ultimately mattered – that was the abyss from which I could easily tumble into madness and despair (and so nearly did).

The problem was that I couldn't find answers to any of my questions. Not satisfactory ones, anyway. So, I just lived with the shame, the anger, and the sense of powerlessness. I did that for many years until I came into my late teens. Then, the anger turned into aggression and violence that, ultimately, led to a prison sentence for serious violent crimes and theft. It was not until I was sat in my prison cell at 21 years of age that I realised just how angry I was. Why was I like this? Why was I so full of rage? Largely, I reflected, because of the injustice I felt at it all. Life wasn't fair, and it certainly hadn't been fair to me.

If there was no God and no hope of justice, then I was merely a helpless victim. A statistic. A casualty of this cruel, godless world.

And that just made me feel worse.

In my mind, there was nothing out there in the universe looking out for me. I had to get on with my life and make the best hand out of the cards dealt to me. The reality was that I was slowly but surely destroying myself from the inside out. I was getting high, committing serious crimes, and becoming ever more violent and out of control. The irony was that the higher I got, the lower I felt. I had little doubt, nor did my court-appointed counsellor, that I would one day commit a more serious crime such as murder. Try as I might, I just couldn't cope with the vast array of emotions that swamped me and threatened to sweep me away.

> I was so *angry.*
> I was so *ashamed.*
> I felt so *guilty.*

I was so *hurt.*

I was so *afraid.*

I didn't know where my emotions were most of the time. I lacked the vocabulary to adequately express myself. That just compounded my helplessness and frustration all the more. The rage I felt was so intense, I could literally feel it aching inside my chest. Sometimes, it overwhelmed me so much that I needed an outlet – any outlet – to set it free.

Usually that meant violence or drugs.

Often both.

This would satisfy my anger, at least for a time. It would help me to temporarily forget. But, when I came back to reality after whatever high I happened to be on, the aching returned, pulsating as strongly as ever. Try as I might, I was forced to carry on with my life as if the abuse I suffered had never even happened.

The world never stopped to commiserate with me.

The world never asked how I was feeling.

The situation was even worse as soon as I realised that the people around me were just as lost and hopeless as I was. Many of them had suffered at the hands of abusers. Many of them had been traumatised into silence. As if by not talking about it we could somehow wipe it from our memory banks. They didn't look for any meaning in their suffering because they didn't believe that there was any to be found.

They didn't have any answers to explain the meaning of life, and they certainly didn't want to hear about my suffering. To even acknowledge it would be to open the floodgates of their own souls. So, the world around me told me that there were no answers. It told me that life was pointless.

You were abused? That's a shame. But it's done now, so get on with it. There was nobody to turn to. Nowhere to process my emotions. All that was left was to turn all of my rage, guilt, shame, and fear in on myself. To spiral into a cycle of self-loathing and recrimination and, in turn, to spew all of that onto society around me.

Especially those in positions of authority.

> Then one day, completely out of the blue, my thoughts came back to God.

WHAT'S GOD GOT TO DO WITH IT?

I hadn't meant to turn to God.

Indeed I hadn't thought about God for a long time. I was at the end of my tether, I suppose. By my late teens and early 20's, I was suffering from terrible panic attacks and taking all sorts of street drugs. I think I was in someone's house and I saw that they had a Bible. I didn't say anything. I just looked at it. It looked so out of place on a table filled with used needles, burnt spoons, tin foil, and all the other drug paraphernalia scattered around the room.

As I sat there, probably high, my mind drifted onto thinking about God. As I looked at that Bible, I began to question myself. *What if God did exist? What if God could help me?* I certainly hadn't helped myself up to this point. My friends were just as bad, if not worse, and had brought not one ounce of inner peace to my life. *What if the Bible was true? What if this life was not the end? What if – and I was far too scared to follow this thought through – everything I had been through was not meaningless?*

I chided myself for even thinking that way. To open that door would be to open myself up to the possibility of hope. Of meaning. Of purpose. And I was too battle-scarred and scared to go down that road again. Where had hope gotten me as a child? Why would God help me as a drug-fuelled, violent criminal when He hadn't helped me as a helpless child – mercilessly terrorised by ruthless, soulless tormentors?

I didn't know it then, but that was the beginning of a long road to faith in Jesus Christ.[1] As I write these words, 24 years after coming to faith, I'd like to share with you the deep meaning and answers that I have found in my pain and suffering. I have been a pastor for almost 20 years. I have studied theology at a very high level. I have preached at least a thousand sermons. I have read the Bible cover to cover countless times. I have prayed. I have cried. I have sought God for understanding and insight. And all of these things have left me with this answer when it comes to the question of why the Lord permitted me to suffer through those childhood agonies.

I just do not know.

Disappointing, right? A bit of an anti-climax. I mean, books like these are meant to give us the steps to heaven. They're meant to tie up all of our troubles in a neat, little God-shaped bow. Don't get me wrong, lots of Christians try to answer questions like this. Here are some of the things that I've heard, and that have been said to me, by well-meaning Christians over the years:

> *God uses our troubles for our own good.*
> *Maybe God was using your trial(s) to discipline you and teach you a lesson.*
> *Maybe you didn't pray with the right motives.*

---

[1]   For a fuller explanation for this please refer to my autobiography, *Is There Anybody Out There? A Journey From Despair To Hope* (Ross-Shire: Christian Focus Publications, 2015).

Maybe there was sin in your life and that's why God didn't answer your prayers.

Maybe God did answer you, but you just didn't hear Him or it wasn't the answer you wanted.

We don't know the answers, but we know that God works all things together for good.

I did not find a single one of them the remotest bit satisfying intellectually nor comforting pastorally.

Instead, the best, and most honest, answer I ever received was from a Christian friend who heard my story, listened to my pain, sighed, hugged me, and said:

I haven't got a clue, Mez. Not a clue.

So, this is a book for those of us who haven't got a clue why we have suffered terrible traumas in our lives, either as children or adults.

This is a book that has no easy answers and will offer none.

This is a book that tries to get behind the tough questions of why God permits such abuses to occur in this world.

So, allow me to walk hand in hand with you as we search together for some sort of meaning, some sort of justice and, maybe, just maybe, answers to some of the terrible pain and traumas we have faced in our lives.

Oh, just one more thing before we dive in. I am going to assume the existence of God for the purposes of this little book.

Now, you don't have to believe in Him at this point. I respect that. I even sympathise if that's your position. But, if we want to think about the spiritual answers to our questions, then let's assume that He does exist. Let's assume the Bible really is God's Word to the human race.

Because, if we make these two assumptions, we can then begin to really question Him about our suffering and our pain.

I WISH MY LIFE WERE BETTER

Sometimes, when I was little, I would dream about a better life. I would sit on the windowsill of my bedroom window and look at the children playing outside on the streets below. Sometimes I would see them walking to the shops holding their mum or dad's hand. And I would wonder what it would be like to have a mum who held my hand and took me to the shop. To have them tell me they love me and buy me sweets.

I'd wish my life was different; better.

When I got older, I would walk down the street and see young children looking out at me from their windows. They would smile and wave, and I would think back to my own childhood. I'd wonder what it would be like to have lived a childhood with toys and love and happiness.

I'd wish my life had been different; better.

As a father of two children I sometimes look at my children larking around, laughing and enjoying life. Pleased as I am for them, I sometimes feel a jolt of pain, of regret for a life I've never had.

I've often wished my start in life had been better.

I suppose we never get tired of wanting life to be better.

Of wanting a better past and a better future.

Instead, we are often stuck with the painful reality of now. This messy thing that we call life.

IT WASN'T ALWAYS LIKE THIS

I mean, you know, we don't live in a perfect world.
(Michael Bloomberg)

Whatever we feel about God, or not, we all want the world to be a better place. We all, at some time or other, wish our lives had been different than what they are, or have been. Maybe we wish we'd known our parents. Maybe we wish that they'd loved us. Maybe we wish we'd had a house full of love instead of shouting and screaming. Maybe we wish that we'd had presents at Christmas instead of hearing our dad's feeble excuses as he blew all his money in the betting shop again. Maybe we wish for life to be pain-free, trouble-free, and war-free. Maybe we wish we could end the suffering of innocent people, especially children.

These are the kinds of wishes for a world that most of us (except the particularly evil ones) could get behind.

And here's the thing: This is the way the world used to be. This is the way God created the world. The Bible teaches us in the very first book – Genesis – that when God created the world, it was completely perfect. Think about that for a minute. According to the Bible, there was a time in the history of our planet when there was no

> *Pain*
> *Suffering*
> *Abuse*
> *Terror*
> *Hate*
> *Shame*
> *Death*

Genesis 1:31 tells us, 'God saw all that he had made, and it was very good.' In this place of perfection, the Garden of Eden, men and women and all of the animal kingdom lived in perfect peace, side by side. There was no bloodshed, no tears, and certainly no abuse. Adam and Eve knew true peace and harmony. Adam didn't choke her out for not cooking his food properly. Eve didn't wrap a bat around his head for losing all his money on gambling. There was no screaming and hurling insults at one another. There was no bringing up past wrongs. There was no baggage from previous, disastrous relationships. There was no paranoia.

Humanity lived in perfect relationship with one another and, more importantly, with Almighty God, their creator.

The world many of us dream about was, in fact, a reality at the dawn of time. But the thought of it is just so incredible, so beyond our human experience, that it not only seems unlikely but unimaginable. We've been caught up in a world of pain for so long that we cannot picture such perfection in our minds.

The chaos of the Big Bang creation myth is far more believable because it resonates with the unfeeling, impersonal suffering of our everyday existence.

But, we need to know that the world was not always like this. Our lives were not always like this.

The dreams we have for a perfect life, a better life, are actually faint echoes of the experience of our ancestors, imprinted into our souls by the God who created us. We want a better life, because deep in our being we know the human race used to run free and happy in the Garden of Eden.

So, how did we get here?
Where did it all go wrong?

REBELLION

I'd always thought of myself as a victim growing up. You know, bad people doing bad stuff to me. But I wasn't bad. I was a good boy. I was innocent. That's how I liked to think of myself. I was a passenger on the train of life; passive.

That's until I discovered another side of my character I didn't know existed. Who knows how old I was. 10? Maybe. 11? Possibly. All I know is that it was just after another round of beatings. This time, it was with a wooden broom handle. I can't remember what it was for. **She** never needed a reason and **she** always found an excuse. The dishes hadn't been washed, or dried, or stacked correctly in the cupboard. I was late home from school. I got 95% in a test instead of 100%. I hadn't changed the television channel quickly enough.

Take your pick.

It didn't matter. I soon worked out that I was getting beaten whatever I did. Not long after that, I discovered that **she** liked it. I mean, really liked it. Some part of her got perverse pleasure from seeing my fear and hearing my pathetic cries for mercy. **She** got off on my pain. So, one day I decided to just take it.

Wordlessly. Soundlessly.

She would beat me, and I would just stand there. **She** would knock me to the ground and I would just lie there. I didn't say a word. I didn't shed a tear. I just stopped altogether.

And **she** hated it. **She** beat me more. **She** beat me harder. **She** starved me. 'You eat nothing until you beg me!' **She** would scream. I would starve. **She** would become more frustrated. **She** took to putting food on the floor and making me eat it. No knife and fork. Just with my mouth. I did it.

Silently and without complaint.

She would smash my head on the floor and rub my face in it. But I continued in my silent rebellion.

I don't know where it came from, but once I found my rebellious streak it stuck with me. **She** could beat me, starve me and abuse me, but I would rebel, even if it was just silent protest, at every occasion. It brought me great pain and suffering – but it also brought me sweet joy and a sense of victory so joyous that, in the end, I looked forward to our battle of wills.

One thing was for sure. I wasn't just a victim anymore.

I was a rebel. And, what's more, I was proud of it.

WILD AT HEART

There's a rebel lying deep in my soul.
(Clint Eastwood)

We are all rebels at heart if we think about it. Almost from the moment we took our first steps, we were hardwired to rebel. If an adult said, 'Don't touch,' we touched. If a place was off limits, we'd have to try to enter. If the sign read, 'No dive bombing' in the local swimming pool, guess what we'd do at the first opportunity when the lifeguard turned their back?

Why?

Why do we do these things? What do we get from it? What's the pay-off? Maybe it's the gratification of getting one over on 'the man' or on other figures of authority? For me, in the dark, lonely hours of my abuse, it was my fist-shake at the world, at my chief tormentor, and at a God I didn't believe in. It was my way of letting the universe know that I wasn't going down without a fight. In later years, when there was no more abuse, I just enjoyed my rebellion. I had become used to it. I had grown comfortable with it. I enjoyed stealing. I enjoyed hitting other people, especially those whom I felt deserved it. I enjoyed breaking the law. It gave me pleasure. It gave me a sense of control and power over my world; all the things I'd never had as a child.

I soon discovered I didn't have to practice my rebellion. It came naturally to me.

If we're honest, rebellion comes naturally to all of us.

Believe it or not, the Bible even has an explanation for this! The Bible has the answer to why we are rebels by nature. Ultimately, it has an answer to why the world is the way it is.

In fact, it teaches us that rebellion and the problems of our world are very closely linked indeed.

THE DEVIL MADE ME DO IT

> The devil's voice is sweet to hear.
> **(Stephen King)**

We are first introduced to the devil when he comes to Eve in the Garden of Eden in **Genesis 3**. The devil is known by many names in the Bible. The word devil itself means *'false accuser'*, but he is also known as *'Satan'*, which means *'enemy'*. He is also called *'the tempter'*, *'the wicked one'*, *'the ruler of this world'*, *'the father of lies'*, and *'the prince of the power of the air'*, to name but a few. In our world, he is portrayed as a cartoon character with horns and a pitchfork; but in the Bible he is described as *'an angel of light'*. He is pictured as *'a dragon'* and we read that he appeared to Eve in the Garden of Eden as *'a serpent'*.

We know that at some point the devil was a powerful angel in heaven with God. He was created by God before the world was created, but at some point pride crept into his heart and he desired to be like God. This is how the prophet Isaiah puts it in **Isaiah 14:12-14 (ESV)**: *'How you are fallen from heaven, O Day Star,* *son of Dawn! How you are cut down to the ground, you who laid the nations low! You said in your heart, "I will ascend to heaven; above the stars of God I will set my throne on high; I will sit on the mount of assembly in the far reaches of the north; I will ascend above the heights of the clouds; I will make myself like the Most High."'*

Even though the devil was the most beautiful of God's angels and had everything he needed in heaven, he wanted more. He wanted total control. He wanted to be number one. Instead, we read later on in **Ezekiel 28:16-17a (ESV)**, *'You were filled with violence in your midst, and you sinned; so I cast you as a profane thing from the mountain of God, and I destroyed you, O guardian cherub, from the midst of the stones of fire. Your heart was proud because of your beauty; you corrupted your wisdom for the sake of your splendour. I cast you to the ground.'*

In other words, Satan gets his marching orders. He is cast out of the presence of God, and in his evil desperation to mess everything up, he turns his attention to the human race.

This leads us to a second, great rebellion.

PATIENT ZERO

As we've already discovered, when God created the first humans – Adam and Eve – He put them within a perfect paradise, the Garden of Eden. There was no pain. There was no suffering. There was no evil. There was just perfection. True communion between humanity and God.

They were given one clear command from God: *'Do not eat from the tree of the knowledge of good and evil.'* That's it. Nothing too complicated. The human race was created to worship God and obey His commandments. Do that and all would be well. Unfortunately, Satan had other ideas. This is what we read about him in **Genesis 3:1-7 (ESV)**.

> *Now the serpent was more crafty than any other beast of the field that the Lord God had made.*
>
> *He said to the woman, 'Did God actually say, "You shall not eat of any tree in the garden"?' And the woman said to the serpent, 'We may eat of the fruit of the trees in the garden, but God said, "You shall not eat of the fruit of the tree that is in the midst of the garden, neither shall you touch it, lest you die."' But the serpent*

said to the woman, 'You will not surely die. For God knows that when you eat of it your eyes will be opened, and you will be like God, knowing good and evil.' So when the woman saw that the tree was good for food, and that it was a delight to the eyes, and that the tree was to be desired to make one wise, she took of its fruit and ate, and she also gave some to her husband who was with her, and he ate. Then the eyes of both were opened, and they knew that they were naked. And they sewed fig leaves together and made themselves loincloths.

Notice that sin enters the world through Adam. Sin didn't originate with Adam. It originally came from the devil. If we think of the devil as the drug cartel boss, then Adam was the drug mule. He was the one who brought sin in over the border and into our world. Or think of it another way. In the 80s and 90s when AIDS was at epidemic levels, scientists were desperately searching for what they called Patient Zero. In other words: the first case. The starting point. They figured that if they could find him or her, then they would be better able to work a cure for the disease.

They never did find out.

Well, Adam is sin's Patient Zero. We can trace back the original source for everything that is wrong with our world. We can trace it back to where it all went so tragically wrong for us. Adam & Eve had one simple job: *Do not eat from that tree.* They had a Paradise to choose from, but we know how the story goes. They ate from the tree and from that exact moment, sin entered the world.

And fast on its heels came a whole world of trouble.

Note that *sin* entered the world, not *sins*. So, adultery or murder or cheating or greed didn't come in with Adam's sin. What came in was the spirit of rebellion against God. When Adam and Eve fell, our spiritual DNA was changed forever. We became sinners by nature. Even in the womb. **Psalm 58:3** puts it like this: '*Even from birth the wicked go astray; from the womb they are wayward, spreading lies.*' That means even babies in the womb are a hotbed of sin and rebellion!

If you think that's a bit harsh, then consider this from the Minnesota Crime Commission, published in 1926:

> *Every baby starts life as a little savage. He is completely selfish and self-centred. He wants what he wants when he wants it – his bottle, his mother's attention, his playmate's toy, his uncle's watch. Deny him these wants, and he seethes with rage and aggressiveness, which would be murderous, were he not so helpless. He is dirty. He has no morals, no knowledge, no skills. This means that all children, not just certain children, are born delinquent. If permitted to continue in the self-centred world of his infancy, given free rein to his impulsive actions to satisfy his wants, every child would grow up a criminal, a thief, a killer, a rapist.*

Shocking, right? But, when we come to understand the Christian's view of the world, we begin to understand the philosophical *why* of child abuse (any abuse), even if we can't quite get to grips with the motivation of each individual's heart. The point is that the whole human race carries the trait of being a sinner, which we got from our first parents, Adam and Eve. Because of them, each of us is born with an inbuilt desire to sin. Some of us like porn. Some of us love money. Some of are full of pride. Some of us are people-pleasers. Some of us are terrible gossips. Some of us like to pump drugs or alcohol into our bodies. Some of us are pimps. Some of us are child abusers.

All of us are born slaves to our desires.

All of us are born sinners.

And the problem is serious.

Because sin has real power, it reigns; it controls and, ultimately, it destroys. We are foolish creatures because we underestimate it. We think we are the ones with all the power and the control. We are not. Our sinful nature runs away with us. It leads us down dangerous and foolish paths.

Unfortunately, in this world of ours, we are not scared enough of our sin and we have no real comprehension of what each of us is truly capable of, were we left to our own selfish desires. Therefore, biblically speaking, we shouldn't be surprised when we turn on the news and see reports of complete and total barbarity around the world. People being trafficked, children being murdered, elderly people being beaten for a few pounds. Sin is a deadly poison and it is to be found in every human heart, every human relationship, every street, every town, every city, and every country all over the world.

All of it can be traced back to Adam: Patient Zero for the entire human race.

If that wasn't bad enough, there is worse news to come...

God holds each of us as responsible for Adam's sin as Adam himself.

IT WASN'T ME

How can God hold us responsible for the sin of two people thousands of years ago? How is that fair? We weren't even there! How can any of us be responsible for something we didn't do?

It would be like my wife, Miriam, being caught speeding (again) and then me and our two daughters receiving a fine in the post. The judge declares that because of her law-breaking, all the family are held responsible too. Would that be fair? No. The girls and I didn't do anything wrong. Why should we pay for my wife's crime? She is responsible for her own behaviour and we are for ours. That's how it should work, right?

Here's how the Bible presents it in **Romans 5:18-19**.

Consequently, just as one trespass resulted in condemnation for all people, so also one righteous act resulted in justification and life for all people. For just as through the disobedience of the one man the many were made sinners, so also through the obedience of the one man the many will be made righteous.

Did you catch that? *Through the one sin (Adam's) we all now stand condemned*. Through the disobedience of one man, *the many* were made sinners. There it is in black and white. I am not asking you to believe it at this stage, but just to accept that this is what the Bible teaches. When Paul says the whole human race are *'made sinners'*, he means that we have been appointed as sinners. God looks at all of the human race as sinners because of Adam. Again, how is this in any way fair to us?

Let's think about the issue another way. Imagine that you are appointed the UK ambassador to China. What would that mean in practice? Well, to be an ambassador for the UK means to represent the entire country and act on behalf of its subjects, and in their best interests. The idea is the same here. Does the ambassador ask every individual person in the UK what they want? No, of course not. The ambassador acts on our behalf, whether we like it or not and whether we agree with them or not. When Adam was created he was the ambassador for the entire human race.

When Adam made his decision to rebel, he made his decision for all of us: God appointed Adam as the representative of the human race. He was told plainly, *as our representative,* that if he disobeyed God he would die, and that we who follow him would die also.

> Adam sinned and, therefore, *we all sinned.*

> That decision led to carnage.

DEATH REIGNS

For the wages of sin is death....
(Romans 6:22a)

ENGLAND, 1980

*Granddad was stumbling around the living room today. I say Granddad, but it's **her** dad. He was staggering about, and all the family was laughing at him.*

Suddenly, he just slumped down on the floor. The laughing stopped. He was dead. Gone. Just like that. We thought he was drunk, but he was having a massive heart attack.

Death reigns.

ENGLAND, 1984

My social worker is dead.

*I've known him for a couple of years. He comes around the house from time to time to check up on me. I can always tell when he is coming because **she** is nice to me. But, as soon as he leaves, **she's** back to normal.*

I liked him a lot. He always used to encourage me and tell me that I could do anything with my life. That I wasn't stupid and useless. That I shouldn't give up. That I should keep studying hard and one day I would escape all of this.

But now, he's gone and killed himself. He stuck a pipe from his exhaust into his car window and now he's dead.

How can I believe a single word he said to me now?

Death reigns.

ENGLAND, 1987
I just found out that Val is dead. Dead! At 15. I can't believe it. I'd just shared a smoke and a joke with him not one hour before.

News shot around the estate. His girlfriend did it. Val was a 'good lad' but he did have a habit of knocking his girlfriends about. This one obviously got fed up and stuck a bread knife in his chest.

I heard that he bled to death in the back of a friend's car on the way to the hospital. That night we smashed every window in her family's house and ran them off the estate.

Death reigns.

My own two children. Dead before they even had a chance at life.

Death reigns.

'*Death Reigns.*' Two of the scariest words in the English language. The Bible teaches us that death reigned from the moment Adam sinned. It reigns still. In fact, sin not only broke into our lives and hearts, it kicked open the door and death swarmed through behind it. Every living thing in the universe is now subject to death. There is no escaping its clutches.

This is how **James 4:14** puts it: '*What is your life? You are a mist that appears for a little while and then vanishes.*' Death has no friends. It plays no favourites. It does not discriminate. The good die along with the evil. The young and the old. The fat and the thin. The rich and the poor.

> The abused.
> The abuser.

We all face the same fate. Some of us will live for a long time. Some of us won't. *Why do we have to die? Why do we have to suffer? What is death even all about?* It just seems so unfair. When we read about Adam & Eve in Genesis, they are living happily in the Garden of Eden.

> No troubles.
> No worries.
> No fear.
> No death.

Then Adam makes one foolish decision and the whole thing goes up in smoke. That one act of willful disobedience lies at the root of all of our problems in the world today.

> All of the suffering.
> All of the pain.

All of the torment.
All of the death.

But it gets even worse.

INNOCENTS LOST

I felt my throat tighten and constrict. My heart ached with
a pain I could not describe. I wondered if I were dying.
I felt not sadness. I felt pity. For myself. For us all. We
were children no longer. And we never would be again.

(K. A. Applegate)

In the exact moment that Adam and Eve sinned, they
lost all of their innocence. Before the fall, they had been
naked before each other and God, and they'd felt no shame
or discomfort in it. But something happened to their minds
when they ate that forbidden fruit.

This is how Paul puts it in **Romans 1:28 CSB**, '*And because
they* [the pagans] *did not think it worthwhile to acknowledge God,
God delivered them over to a corrupt mind so that they do what is not
right.*' He says a similar thing in **2 Corinthians 4:4**, '*The god of this
age* [Satan] *has blinded the minds of unbelievers so that they cannot
see the light of the Gospel that displays the glory of Christ, who is the
image of God.*' Since the fall of the human race all those years ago,
the Bible teaches us that the mind of the world is hostile to God,
spiritually dark and depraved.

In fact, it doesn't take very long from the fall in **Genesis 3** to the first murder in **Genesis 4**. Just two chapters after that, we read that the whole earth was filled with violence. Then we have story after story and book after book in the Bible which lists all the terrible things humans began to do to one another as sin took its terrible toll on the human race.

Nothing was out of bounds.

Incest, bestiality, child sacrifice.

It's all there in black and white. The whole ugly, dark, corrupted minds and hearts of the human race laid bare for us to see. The truly scary thing is that instead of being a book, the Bible is, in fact, more like a mirror. Once we open it up, we begin to see our true nature reflected in it. We begin to realise that we, too, in the deep, dark recesses of our souls, are more than capable of untold horrors against the rest of humanity. One truth jumps out at us again and again:

We are all sinners.

So, if we think about it, the Bible actually offers us a clear reason as to why the world is the way it is. It helps us to understand why parents abuse their children, and why people commit unspeakable acts of evil and cruelty against one another.

When sin entered the world, death came with it and all our original sense of holy innocence was lost.

IT WON'T ALWAYS BE LIKE THIS

See, I will create
new heavens and a new earth.
The former things will not be remembered,
nor will they come to mind.
(Isaiah 65:17)

The last book of the Bible is called *Revelation* and in that book we are told that one day Jesus is coming back and He is going to bring an end to this world. On that fateful day God will judge the world on the basis of who has faith in Jesus and who does not. This is what **Revelation 21:1-5** tells us about this great day that will one day come.

> *Then I saw 'a new heaven and a new earth,' for the first heaven and the first earth had passed away, and there was no longer any sea. I saw the Holy City, the new Jerusalem, coming down out of heaven from God, prepared as a bride beautifully dressed for her husband. And I heard a loud voice from the throne saying, 'Look! God's dwelling place is now among the people, and he will dwell with them. They will be his people, and God himself will be with*

*them and be their God. He will wipe every tear from their eyes.
There will be no more death or mourning or crying or pain, for the
old order of things has passed away.' He who was seated on the
throne said, 'I am making everything new!'*

The promise here is that one day, God is going to make all things
new. In other words, one day there will be a return to the Garden
of Eden. We are going to go back to how things used to be. One
day, life will be perfect once again and the human race will exist
in peace with one another and will live in perfect relationship
with God.

For eternity.

Here's the problem: *It all sounds so pie-in-the-sky. So what, we think,
the world used to be perfect. It isn't anymore, is it? So what, we think,
one day it will be perfect again. That doesn't change the complete chaos
of this life, does it?*

So, where does all this leave us? The problem is, we can't turn
the clock back to the perfection of Eden and we cannot travel
forward in time to the glory and beauty of this new heaven and
new earth.

We are forced, then, to live in the angry, violent, abusive mess
of our present reality. Trapped between what used to be in some
distant past and what might again be in some distant future.

LIFE IN THE MESSY MIDDLE

Our world today so desperately hungers for hope, yet uncounted people have almost given up. There is despair and hopelessness on every hand.

(Billy Graham)

It's one thing to hear of a perfect couple in a perfect world and of a future of unending joy and peace. It's quite another to live in the mess and chaos of our own time and place. We live in what I call the messy middle; we live between the times. The perfect world that used to be is long since gone, and the one that's meant to be coming seems like a pipe dream to many of us. Instead, we live in the time when:

> Parents *abuse* their children.
> Parents *abandon* their children.
> Children *hurt* one another.
> Teenagers *kill* one another.
> People commit *suicide*.

We live in a time when people are capable of unspeakable acts against one another. We live in a terrible world; one spoiled by great evil and the selfishness of the human race.

As I've argued, the Bible puts it down to sin entering the world, through the devil, which has led to a history of rebellion and catastrophe for our planet. So, if the Bible is true (and I believe it is), then this throws up a whole raft of questions:

> *Why is God allowing all this to happen?*
> *What is going on? Is He asleep at the wheel?*
> *Does He not see the pain and the misery?*
> *Why doesn't He do something about it?*
> *If He is so loving, why is He letting innocents suffer?*
>
> *Why doesn't He just intervene?*

Well, there is some good news.

God *has* stepped in.
God *has* intervened.

Just not in the way that we would expect.
Or even want.

For God so loved the world that he gave his one and only son....
(John 3:16)

CONSIDER JESUS

Consider him....
(Hebrews 12:3)

The Bible encourages us to do one very important thing with Jesus: *Consider Him*, we are commanded.

Consider *Him*. In other words, take some time out of your life and really think about Jesus. Yes, we want answers to our questions. Yes, we want to find some meaning from (or despite) our pain and suffering. Yes, we want justice. Think about how many sleepless nights we have had thinking about all of the bad things that have happened to us. We've looked at them from every angle. We've tried to figure out every motivation. *Why did the person or people do it? Why did others let them do it? Which family members knew about it and which ones didn't?*

Let's take some time to consider Jesus and the claims *He* makes. I know the name of Jesus doesn't mean much to many of us these days. We may have a vague notion about Him, but nothing concrete. When I was a child, Jesus was more like a Father Christmas figure. A sort of imaginary, fantasy person who was probably a good bloke but had no connection to my life and my problems. But the Bible paints a very different picture of Jesus. It tells us that He wasn't just a nice teacher who was kind to people and loved puppies.

He is so much more than that.

In fact, when we get to the heart of who Jesus was and what He did, we get to the heart of how God feels about our suffering, our pain, and our shame.

The Bible teaches us two clear truths about who Jesus is.

TRUTH NUMBER 1

Jesus is fully God.

Lots of books have been written on this subject in the past two thousand years, and I have no wish to rehash things here.[1] The Bible makes it clear that Jesus was God come to earth. Writing to Titus in **Titus 2:13**, Paul calls Jesus *'our great God and saviour.'* The Apostle John, after seeing Jesus post-resurrection, falls at His feet and cries out in **John 20:28**, *'My Lord and my God.'*

This is the reason Jesus is so controversial. Because when we do begin to consider Him, we soon discover that He made outrageous statements about Himself. In **John 8,** Jesus is debating His nature with Jewish opponents. He declares to them in verse **58**, *'Before Abraham was, I am.'* In effect, He tells them, *'I am eternal. I was never created. I am God.'* And we know that this is precisely what He meant, because of their reaction to this statement in verse **59**: *'At this, they picked up stones to stone him.'* The Apostle Paul is even more direct as he teaches the church in

---

1   In my book, *God: Is He Out There?* (Ross-Shire: CFP, 2016), I talk about Jesus more fully.

Colossians 1:16, *'For in him* [Jesus] *all things were created: things in heaven and on earth, visible and invisible, whether thrones or powers or rulers or authorities; all things have been created through him and for him.'*

Jesus is, always has been, and eternally will be, God.

That's an important truth to establish as we move on in our search for answers to our own issues.

In the Christian church, we teach that God is a Trinity and He exists as three distinct persons: *Father, Son, & Holy Spirit.*

> The *Father* is **God.**
> The *Son* is **God.**
> The *Holy Spirit* is **God.**

Each of these three persons is equally God. They are equal in power, love, mercy, justice, holiness, knowledge, and all other qualities. Yet each of them is distinct from one another and relates to one another.

God is not divided into three equal parts.
There is only one God.

All three are equally and personally divine, yet share one essence.

Yes, I know this is head-scratchingly heavy stuff. But please stick with me. It's important we get a right understanding of God if we are to consider Jesus properly. You see, not only did the early church recognise Jesus as God, but Jesus made these claims of Himself in **John 10:30** when He says, *'I and the Father are one'*. In **John 12:44** He is even bolder when He announces to the gathered crowd that *'whoever believes in me believes in him who sent me'*.

Jesus claims what no other leader of any religion has ever said about themselves. All the other prophets and leaders claimed to know how to get to the truth, or to show us a better way to live. But not Jesus. He says in **John 14:6**, *'I am the way and the truth and the life. No one comes to the Father except through me.'* In other words, He's not like some lifestyle guru. He did not come to show us a better way or to even help us find God.

HE IS GOD

And He says that He has come to find us.

Therefore, in our search for meaning and purpose, we need to understand that all faiths do not lead us to God. All religious leaders are not the same. In fact, Jesus stands alone among all other religious leaders in the world, particularly with regard to *the claims He makes about Himself.*

That's why the world either loves Him or hates Him. We can't respect Jesus' teachings and not believe in Him. That's why He was murdered on a cross. That's why the ordinary people loved Him, but the religious establishment despised Him.

Jesus claimed to be God. *Consider Him*, the Bible says. *Consider that claim.* We cannot be indifferent to Jesus and what He claims about Himself. If we are indifferent to the Christian faith and the claims of Jesus, then we've clearly not understood Him.

Jesus is the great I AM. He is God.

Therefore, if we want to know what God is like and what God thinks about us and all of the pain we have been through, then we need look no further than Jesus. He will show us and reveal to us everything we need to know, as well as many things we don't want to hear! Remember, *when Jesus speaks, God speaks*. And, incredibly, He wants to speak to us.

> If this news wasn't incredible enough…
> There's more.

TRUTH NUMBER 2

> *Jesus is fully man*

There has *never* been a time when Jesus was not God. But there *was* a time when He was not a man. The Bible teaches us that He *became* a man 2,000 years ago. We must be clear that when Jesus came to earth, He didn't stop being God the Son. He remained fully God as He became fully man in the flesh.

This is how the Apostle John puts it in **John 1:1**. *'In the beginning was the Word, and the Word was with God, and the Word was God.'* The *Word* being spoken of here is Jesus. Look at what John goes on to say about it in **John 1:14**: *'And the Word was made flesh.* ***And the Word dwelt among us****. He was full of grace and truth.'*

Jesus really was born as a baby. He really did suffer all the trials of being a human being as we do. He really was tempted by the devil as we are. He really did identify with us in every single way possible. This wasn't God merely pretending to be a man. He really walked the earth 2,000 years ago.

> *Yet, He was without sin.*
> *Perfect in every single way.*

We need to get our heads around this because what this means for those of us who have suffered is that God has not been indifferent to us. Nor can we claim that God doesn't understand what we've been through. He's so concerned about us that He came to earth.

And He loves us so much that He went to extraordinary lengths to prove it.

This has massive ramifications for us in terms of our pain and suffering. Because God, in Jesus, has lived among us, He knows full well what it is like to live in the messy, painful chaos of our fallen world.

> He knows our suffering because He has suffered too.

> In fact, Jesus has suffered far more than we could ever hope to appreciate.

This is the Jesus I am asking you to consider. *Fully God* and *Fully Man*. Jesus, who came to earth to live in a run-down, poky little town in Israel some 2,000 years ago. No social media, none of the scientific advances of our day. A backwater town in a nation that had seen better days.

Consider this Jesus. Just for a few more pages. Just for a few more hours of your life.

Maybe you're thinking:

> *'Why should I consider Him? What's He ever done for me? He never considered me when I was being abused.'*

That's OK.

Again, I can fully understand that. But, I think in considering Jesus and the claims He makes, we can find a way through the anger, the grief, and the shame that we feel for a childhood lost or self-respect stolen from us.

Because what's really telling when we're asked to consider Jesus the God-Man, is the reason given for why we should spend our time doing so.

JESUS CAME TO DIE

He endured such opposition from sinners.
(Hebrews 12:3)

When Jesus came to earth, yes, the angels sang about it; yes, the wise men came and brought gifts to Him; yes, the shepherds rejoiced. But that was about it. There were no red carpets. There was no great party to mark the occasion. No visiting dignitaries came calling. In fact, one king, Herod, was desperately trying to track Him down so that he could murder Him.

Jesus, the God-man, was born in squalor, surrounded by animals and their dung. There was nothing romantic about the scene in the slightest. The single greatest event in the history of the world and there were no TV cameras to record it. No reporters beating down Joseph's door looking for a quote.

Sometimes we ask what God has done for us when the real question is *what more could He do!*

Jesus has come to earth.

God has come to earth.

He entered into our broken, chaotic, painfully messy reality. This means that He is not a God who is far off, disinterested in us. He is a God who has come near to us. That's why He was given the name *Immanuel*, which literally means *God with us*.

Imagine how He could have come. All thunder and lightning. Rolling back the heavens and revealing His full glory. Drying up the waters of the earth that He had made. Leading an army of untold millions of warrior angels to claim His rightful property. But there was none of that. Instead, this is how Paul describes it in **Philippians 2:6-8**: *'Who* [Jesus], *being in very nature God, did not consider equality with God something to be used to his own advantage; rather, he made himself nothing by taking the very nature of a servant, being made in human likeness. And being found in appearance as a man, he humbled himself by becoming obedient to death – even death on a cross!'*

Jesus gave up the perfect glories of heaven to step into our messy reality. He gave up all His godly, rightful authority and power. He laid aside the indescribable glories of heaven to step into our messed-up reality.

> *What has God ever done for those of us who have suffered?*
> *Why doesn't He help us?*
> *Why didn't He answer our cries for help in our darkest moments?*
> *Why are our abusers allowed to roam about free and easy?*
> *If He's so good and loving, why did He let it all happen to us?*

All of these questions, and more, find their answers in considering Jesus. Let's, just for a moment, consider the God-Man, Jesus, who didn't leave us to our own devices. Who didn't let us stew in our own sin and mess. Who hasn't forgotten about us.

The answer to our questions aren't just found in the fact that He came, they're found in the manner of His coming, His living, His dying and His leaving. It's when we peel back the layers and consider what He went through – how He was abused – and the depths to which He suffered, that we can begin to shine some light in the dark recesses of our own souls.

Jesus, likewise, *endured* suffering.

You might be thinking, *'Well at least Jesus had a family that cared for him. He had Mary & Joseph. That's more than I ever had. At least His family didn't abuse Him and turn Him into a human punchbag.'*

You're right.

He did have a loving family on earth. He also had a perfect community in heaven. But that doesn't mean that Jesus didn't suffer. Far from it. Jesus knows much more than what it means to be human. He knows a suffering so shocking, so profound, that it takes our breath away and leaves us asking not,

Why didn't He help me in my suffering?

But,

Why would He go to such lengths, to suffer so much, for a person like me?

'SUCK IT UP. YOU'RE ON YOUR OWN!'

I can't remember when the pain started. But it was agonising. A hot, searing pain across my stomach. I remember that I was walking back to school from my lunch break and I barely made it through the school gates. I stumbled into my classroom and almost collapsed on the floor.

I was taken to see the headteacher and was given a lift home by one of my teachers. He dropped me off at my front door and I struggled inside. **She** was there. As usual. With a group of her friends. As usual. They were drinking. As usual. 'What are you doing home?' **She** pointed a lit cigarette at my face. 'Have you been bad?' 'No,' I stammered, 'I'm not feeling well. I've got a bad pain in my stomach.' 'You what? A pain in your stomach! You look all right to me.' **She** prods me hard in my belly button and the pain is so excruciating I struggle to stay on my feet. The whole room goes deathly quiet. I scan the assembled faces, looking for sympathy, an ally, anybody, to stand up for me. I shouldn't have bothered. Those that feel uncomfortable with the situation are looking at the floor and refuse to meet my scared, pleading eyes. They are far more worried about her wrath than the pain of a scrawny, underfed 11-year-old boy. 'Stand up straight,' **she** screams. 'Who do you think you're kidding? There's nothing wrong with you.' I didn't see the blow to my head, but I felt it as I was knocked back into the living room door. 'I'll give you a pain in your stomach!'

The last thing I remember was her booted foot coming down on my stomach, and the wild, evil hatred in her eyes as she viciously stamped on me.

Three hours later, I was in an operating theatre having my appendix removed. Apparently, they had panicked when I wouldn't wake up and so were forced to call an ambulance. I later learned that **she** had left me there and had gone to the pub, and so a neighbour had sat with me until the paramedics showed up.

I lay in that hospital bed that night, sobbing quietly to myself, in pain, frightened and alone.

So, so alone.

COMPASSION

noun: *compassion;* **plural noun:** *compassions*

> *sympathetic pity and concern for the sufferings or misfortunes of others.*

synonyms:

> pity, sympathy, feeling, fellow feeling, empathy,
> understanding, care, concern, solicitude, solicitousness,
> sensitivity, tender-heartedness, soft-heartedness,
> warm-heartedness, warmth, love, brotherly love,
> tenderness, gentleness, mercy, mercifulness, leniency,
> lenience, tolerance, consideration, kindness, humanity,
> humaneness, kind-heartedness, charity, benevolence.

THE COMPASSION OF JESUS

For we do not have a high priest who is unable to empathise
with our weaknesses, but we have one who has been
tempted in every way, just as we are—yet he did not sin.
(Hebrews 4:15)

*C*ompassion. We cannot consider Jesus without
considering the word *compassion*. When we read
the New Testament, we see how Jesus traveled around
preaching the good news of the kingdom of God, doing
good deeds, healing the sick, even raising the dead! Yet,
everything He did on earth came out of His compassion
for *the last, the least,* and *the lost.* Consider these various
accounts in the Bible:

> *For we do not have a high priest who is unable to empathise with*
> *our weaknesses, but we have one who has been tempted in every*
> *way, just as we are – yet he did not sin.* **(Hebrews 4:15)**

> *When Jesus heard what had happened, he withdrew by boat*
> *privately to a solitary place. Hearing of this, the crowds followed*
> *him on foot from the towns. When Jesus landed and saw a large*

crowd, **he had compassion on them** *and healed their sick.* **(Matthew 14:13-14)**

Two blind men were sitting by the roadside, and when they heard that Jesus was going by, they shouted, 'Lord, Son of David, have mercy on us!' The crowd rebuked them and told them to be quiet, but they shouted all the louder, 'Lord, Son of David, have mercy on us!' Jesus stopped and called them. 'What do you want me to do for you?' he asked. 'Lord,' they answered, 'we want our sight.' **Jesus had compassion on them** *and touched their eyes. Immediately they received their sight and followed him.* **(Matthew 20:30-34)**

As he approached the town gate, a dead person was being carried out – the only son of his mother, and she was a widow. And a large crowd from the town was with her. When the Lord saw her, **his heart went out to her** *and he said, 'Don't cry.' Then he went up and touched the bier they were carrying him on, and the bearers stood still. He said, 'Young man, I say to you, get up!' The dead man sat up and began to talk, and Jesus gave him back to his mother.* **(Luke 7:12-15)**

Often, the picture in our minds of Jesus forgets His humanity. Yet He hated to see misery and pain. It grieved His very soul to see people suffering, being abused and neglected. In every town and village He visited, His compassion would overspill as He was faced with the almost endless crowds of suffering people. Listen to how Jesus reacts in **Matthew 14:14** as a large crowd descends upon Him. '*When Jesus landed and saw a large crowd,* **he had compassion on them** *and healed their sick*'. Later on in that same passage, Jesus can't bear to see the people hungry and we read of the miracle of the five loaves and two fish.

But we'd be mistaken if we think His compassionate heart was only based on the physical needs of those around Him. Jesus was deeply, deeply concerned for the spiritual state of the people. We read of this in **Matthew 9:36**: *'When he [Jesus] saw the crowds, **he had compassion on them**, because they were harassed and helpless, like sheep without a shepherd.'* The people may have been suffering from all sorts of physical and emotional issues, but Jesus is grieved because of their spiritual state.

The people were spiritually lost.

They were blind to the spiritual state of their souls. They thought their biggest problem was a medical complaint, or the pain of losing a loved one. Who knows how many abused people were in the crowds, suffering silent shame, looking for a bit of love and compassion. Yes, these things are terrible. But, to Jesus, there was something far worse than the agonies of earthly pains: There was the agony of spiritual separation from God the Father.

If physical pain and suffering broke His heart, then the spiritual poverty of the world around Him pierced the very depths of His soul. Look at how He responds to the hard-heartedness of Jerusalem in **Luke 19:41-42**: *'As he approached Jerusalem and saw the city, **he wept over it** and said, "If you, even you, had only known on this day what would bring you peace – but now it is hidden from your eyes."'* There is never an incident recorded in the Bible when Jesus did not respond to the pain and suffering of those He came into contact with. On the contrary, Jesus is reported to have been deeply grieved, often to the point of tears, over the sin and suffering of the people around Him.

I know you're reading this book and your soul aches. Maybe the world and your tormentors have moved on, but you are stuck in your nightmare day after day. Maybe you're still trapped and feel like there is no way out. People don't know. Not really. People don't understand what you've been through. You see a family walking down the road holding hands and it makes you feel sad. You read the newspaper stories of children being abused and the anger wells up inside. You ache for the lack of compassion shown to you or others, as time and people just roll forward, never looking back and never stopping to sympathise. You ache for justice. Sometimes, you don't even know what you ache for. It just hurts. You just want somebody, anybody, to recognise that your pain exists. Even if they can't understand it. Somebody to take you by the hand, look into your eyes and tell you that it is all going to be alright. That what happened to you was not right. In fact, it was evil. You just want a little bit of compassion.

Does Jesus see your pain? Does He feel that aching in your heart?

Yes.

More than that, He is deeply grieved by what has happened to you. The ugly, terrible, global effects of sin bring tears to His eyes. We may feel that He doesn't care or that He's not listening, but He is. That fact that Jesus, the compassionate God-Man, came to earth, is proof that not only is He listening, but He cares. He cares deeply. Our abusers may have lacked compassion, but Jesus does not.

Jesus *knows.*

He **knows.**

His heart aches too. Not just for your pain and mine. Not just for the tragedy of it all. He aches for the loss of a perfect world in Eden. He aches for the loss of peace and love between people.

He aches for the cruelty and inhumanity of our world. He aches for the hideous evil we inflict upon one another. He aches for the powerlessness of the helpless. He aches for the little children hiding under kitchen tables as their mums are beaten to a pulp by drunken, inadequate bullies. He aches for the helpless innocents passed around a paedophile ring. He aches for the man tortured by his wife who is too afraid to speak out because of his shame. He aches for the elderly lady being terrorised by her neighbours. He aches for the sex offender sat in his cell wondering why his life went so wrong.

Jesus really does know.

His heart aches almost until bursting point. For all of these reasons; and for much, much more. His aching reaches its crescendo as He agonises over the state of our souls. There is a reason He chose to come into the messy, chaotic pain of our lives. There is a reason that He weeps bitter tears at the hardness of people's hearts.

We are more lost than we realise. But we're not alone. There is one who sees, and He has compassion on us.

And He is going to go to great lengths to prove it.

HUMILIATION

'*T*ake your clothes off!' she barks. 'No,' I say more defiantly than I feel, 'I don't want to. You can't make me.' Of course she can. She is much older and much bigger than me. She can make me do anything she wants to, and she knows it. Inevitably, she often does.

She's supposed to be my babysitter while my dad and **her** are down the pub. In reality, she's our next-door neighbour who treats my sister and me like personal playthings. She delights in making me run around the house naked. She makes me fondle myself with threats of violence to my sister. She laughs at my confusion and embarrassment at the situation.

Sometimes she takes her own clothes off. Her top at least. She asks me what I think. 'I don't know,' I shrug. That gets me a punch in the face and she grabs my testicles and digs her fingernails in so deep that they break the skin. 'OK. OK.' I wince, too scared to move. 'They're nice.' In truth, I don't know what to say. I'm 10 years old. I just want to go to my room and read a book. She laughs and smacks me across the head.

'Stand there!' she orders, pointing to a spot in the middle of the living room. 'Don't move until I say so.' I stand there, naked, unable to cover up my shame for fear of a beating; shivering and humiliated for the next couple of hours, inwardly praying that it will all be over soon. Of course she smirks to herself, safe in the knowledge that I will never tell. I mean, who could I tell anyway? An absent father, who was either working, drinking or gambling. Or the wicked stepmother who not only said and did far worse things to me, but lacked any compassion whatsoever?

I was on my own, clinging to the vain hope of there being a God out there somewhere who would come to my rescue. Sometimes I wondered if He could see what was happening to me or if He just didn't care.

> Where is God, I would wonder, in those moments of soul-destroying humiliation?

JESUS AND HUMILIATION

The Holy One entered a world of perversion, violence, hatred, suffering, and injustice.

(Al Baker)

If Jesus knows anything at all, He knows intimately what it is like to be publicly humiliated. You don't even have to be a Christian to accept the historical facts of His crucifixion. When Jesus was taken, illegally, by the Jews late at night and tried for blasphemy, we read these words about His accusers in **Matthew 26:67-68**: *'Then they spit in his face and struck him with their fists. Others slapped him and said, "Prophesy to us, Messiah. Who hit you?"'*

But it didn't stop there. The Jewish leaders didn't have the authority to kill Jesus, so they took Him to the only man that could, the Roman governor, Pontius Pilate. **Matthew 27:11-26** records the event for us:

Meanwhile Jesus stood before the governor, and the governor asked him, 'Are you the king of the Jews?' 'You have said so,' Jesus replied. When he was accused by the chief priests and the elders, he gave no answer. Then Pilate asked him, 'Don't you hear the testimony they are bringing against you?' But Jesus made no reply, not even to a single charge – to the great amazement of the governor.

Now it was the governor's custom at the festival to release a prisoner chosen by the crowd. At that time they had a well-known prisoner whose name was Jesus Barabbas. So, when the crowd had gathered, Pilate asked them, 'Which one do you want me to release to you: Jesus Barabbas, or Jesus who is called the Messiah?' For he knew it was out of self-interest that they had handed Jesus over to him.

While Pilate was sitting on the judge's seat, his wife sent him this message: 'Don't have anything to do with that innocent man, for I have suffered a great deal today in a dream because of him.' But the chief priests and the elders persuaded the crowd to ask for Barabbas and to have Jesus executed. 'Which of the two do you want me to release to you?' asked the governor. 'Barabbas,' they answered. 'What shall I do, then, with Jesus who is called the Messiah?' Pilate asked. They all answered, 'Crucify him!' 'Why? What crime has he committed?' asked Pilate.

But they shouted all the louder, 'Crucify him!'

When Pilate saw that he was getting nowhere, but that instead an uproar was starting, he took water and washed his hands in front of the crowd. 'I am innocent of this man's blood,' he said. 'It is your responsibility!' All the people answered, 'His blood is on us and on our children!' Then he released Barabbas to them. But he had Jesus flogged, and handed him over to be crucified.

The perfect, sinless God-Man, wrongly arrested and charged by the Jewish leaders, having been mocked and jeered, was now in the hands of the Roman governor. Notice, Pilate knows that Jesus is not guilty of any crime and yet still he hands Him over to the baying crowd. The injustice of it! The disgrace! The shame!

But, things get worse for Jesus as we read on in **Matthew 27:27-31**: *'Then the governor's soldiers took Jesus into the Praetorium and gathered the whole company of soldiers around him. They stripped him and put a scarlet robe on him, and then twisted together a crown of thorns and set it on his head. They put a staff in his right hand. Then they knelt in front of him and mocked him. "Hail, king of the Jews!" they said. They spit on him and took the staff and struck him on the head again and again. After they had mocked him, they took off the robe and put his own clothes on him. Then they led him away to crucify him.'*

An innocent stripped and beaten and mocked for nothing other than the savage amusement of others. Can you imagine the horror of it? The humiliation?

I remember many years ago when I first considered Jesus and I read these verses. They didn't answer many of my questions, but they did bring me a measure of comfort. Jesus was not indifferent to my humiliation. He had suffered His own, far, far greater than mine.

While I stood naked – my humiliation laid bare before cruel eyes – heaven wept. Jesus grieved as one who had been through His own, deeply painful, humiliating ordeal, naked and bleeding, mocked and despised, at the hands of the very people He had created.

> And for Jesus, there was still far greater suffering and humiliation to come.

REJECTION

There would be no warning. No discussion. The lights would go on in my bedroom and a stranger would come in and order me to dress. 'Why?' I'd ask. The answer was the same every time. 'We are taking you somewhere safe.' 'Where's my dad?' No answer. Wherever he was, he was never there at those times.

She would stay in the kitchen drinking tea and smoking furiously.
No eye contact.
No goodbye.
No reaction to my sister and me being hauled off for what felt like the hundredth time.

I'd given up struggling as I'd done the first few times. There was no point. Looking back now I'm not sure why I struggled when my life was so horrific. Better to be hurt by people you knew than loved by people you didn't. At least in my young mind. That's why I didn't tell on her. That, and the fact that nobody really asked me to be honest. It's not like they ever asked my opinion on anything.

Social workers would stop by once in a while, but I'd been programmed what to say by the promise of a bag of chips and a bar of chocolate. My silence was easily bought. I'd say anything for a day without pain. I'd do anything to make her happy. When **she** was happy, my life was easier. When **she** wasn't, well that was a world of suffering.

I think it was the fear of not knowing. The fear of being around strangers.

> More people to hate me.
> To hurt me.
> To reject me.
>
> Sometimes I cried for my real mother. Why did she leave me with this woman? Why was she letting this happen to me?

My stepmother would regularly stumble into my bedroom in the early hours, stinking of alcohol and stale cigarettes. I'd close my eyes so tight and pretend to be asleep. And **she** would lean in to my ear and whisper, 'She hates you, you know. Your mother. Absolutely despises you. That's why she left you. Because you're useless. You're a nobody. Like your dad. He hates you too. He loves the horses far more than he'll ever love you.' Then **she** would stagger out of the room and I wouldn't breathe or open my eyes until I heard the creak of the mattress next door, as **she** slumped onto her bed.

Then I'd sit on my windowsill and look at the sky and wonder why everybody hated me so much.

I'd wonder if that was why God never helped me, because He hated me too.

JESUS & REJECTION

He came to that which was his own, but his own did not receive him.
(John 1:11)

When Jesus first began His ministry on earth, He wasn't exactly welcomed with open arms. The people in His own hometown rejected Him out of hand. **Mark 6:1-3** records the event for us:

> Jesus left there and went to his hometown, accompanied by his disciples. When the Sabbath came, he began to teach in the synagogue, and many who heard him were amazed. 'Where did this man get these things?' they asked. 'What's this wisdom that has been given him? What are these remarkable miracles he is performing? Isn't this the carpenter? Isn't this Mary's son and the brother of James, Joseph, Judas and Simon? Aren't his sisters here with us?' And they took offence at him.

We read words like these in a flat way. But they were said with a sneer as they looked down upon Jesus: 'The dude's just a carpenter. He's Mary's lad. Who does he think he is?' And so they just rejected

Him out of hand. People He'd known and grown up with. Isn't that one of the most painful rejections of all? And it wasn't just His neighbours. His own family turned their back on Him. In **Mark 3:21**, they accuse Him of being *'out of his mind'*. At other times, people tried to kill Jesus because they just could not accept what He was saying in His claims to be God in the flesh. It's not that people didn't care about what He did and said, it's the fact that they were so dismissive of Him.

We read an account in **Luke 9:51-53** of the Samaritans rejecting Him:

> As the time approached for him to be taken up to heaven, Jesus resolutely set out for Jerusalem. And he sent messengers on ahead, who went into a Samaritan village to get things ready for him; but the people there did not welcome him, because he was heading for Jerusalem.

In other words, they reject Him for being a Jew. And these were people who knew what it was like to be rejected themselves! Everybody hated the Samaritans. They were considered half-breeds for intermarrying with those outside the Jewish faith. They were outcasts. And so the tragedy is that even these people wouldn't have anything to do with Jesus.

Even Peter, one of his closest disciples, who had been with Him since the beginning, even turned his back on Jesus. After Jesus was arrested, Peter was recognised as one of His disciples and when he was challenged about it in **Luke 22:60**, he said, *'Man, I do not know what you are talking about!'* And Peter wasn't the only one. Right at the end, just before He would be crucified, all His disciples scattered and ran.

His neighbours, His friends, religious leaders, His enemies and even His own family rejected Him. **Isaiah 53:3** puts it like this: '*He* [Jesus] *was despised and rejected by mankind, a man of suffering, and familiar with pain. Like one from whom people hide their faces he was despised, and we held him in low esteem.*'

If Jesus knew one thing in this world, He knew what it was like to be rejected. To have the world turn its back on Him either in hostility or indifference.

But here's a promise for you: If you come to Jesus, **He will never reject you**. He will never turn His back on you.

> *All those the Father gives me will come to me, and whoever comes to me I will never drive away.* **(John 6:37)**

That's the cast-iron promise of *His* word.

PAIN & SUFFERING

I hear the first thud before I hear her voice. 'Move it, you stupid spastic!' More thuds follow. Thud! Thud! Thud! I sneak to the top of the landing and peek my head down the stairs. My disabled sister is being dragged by her hair backwards to the hallway below. Who knows what she has done to incur **her** wrath this time.

I'm just glad it isn't me.

She kicks the living room door open and drags my sister through it. My sister isn't struggling. There's no point. That only makes the pain worse, so she just tries to move as quickly as she can so she doesn't lose too many clumps of hair. We've both become pros over the years at trying to minimise the pain as much as we can.

It's the whimpering I can never forget. Like an injured animal by the side of the road. Not screaming out. Not crying. Just whimpering in misery, confusion and pain.

I follow them through the door at a safe distance. I don't want to put myself in the firing line. They're in the kitchen now and my sister has been dragged to the sink. 'What do you call that?' My sister says nothing. Just sobs, softly. 'Answer me!' **she** screams, spittle dripping off her chin. 'A... a... a spoon?' My sister manages to say. 'Well, what's it doing in there?' 'I... I... don't know.' Without warning, **she** slams her head off the edge of the sink, and my sister slides to the floor in a daze. 'You're nothing but a lazy spastic!' **She** boots her in the stomach. 'Get up off that floor and get it washed.'

She turns toward the living room and so I run as fast as I can to my bedroom and silently close the door. A few minutes later I hear the footsteps of my sister, limping back to her room. I hear her door close and then the all-too-familiar sound of muffled crying. She daren't cry too loud in case this makes her angrier still. I want to go and tell her that it's going to be alright. But I know it's not. And I know at some point today it will be my turn to face the rage and feel the sting of whatever torture **she** wants to inflict upon me.

So I do nothing. I sit on my bed, feeling bad for my suffering sister, trembling in terror, crying softly to myself.

Waiting for my turn.

Waiting to hear that all-too-familiar sound of the creaking on the stairs.

JESUS & SUFFERING

But he was pierced for our transgressions, he was crushed for our iniquities; the punishment that brought us peace was on him, and by his wounds we are healed.

(Isaiah 53:5)

By the end of His life Jesus had become well acquainted with pain. We really have no understanding of the pain He went through on the cross. I remember when *The Passion of the Christ*[1] was released in the cinema and many people walked out, upset by the graphic nature of the violence. Crucifixion was a terrible way to die. One of the worst and most evil forms of torture devised by the human race. In Roman times, crucifixion was reserved for the worst of criminals: traitors and murderers.

But, before we get to the cross, we read in **John 19:1** that Pilate handed Jesus over to be flogged. In Jesus' day, floggings were a common thing. Even the Jews had a law on the limit of

---

1   *The Passion of the Christ* was a movie released in 2004 and directed by Mel Gibson.

times that a person could be flogged. For them it was a maximum of 39 times. But the Romans took flogging to a whole other level. They called it scourging and it was *designed purposely* to be as painful as possible. The whips used had at least three straps, each weighted down on the end with either lead balls or animal bones. They were specifically designed to rip open the skin upon contact. They would have stripped Jesus of His clothing, tied Him down and whipped Him mercilessly until He was a bloody pulp.

Again, the whole thing would have been controlled and deliberate. People had been known to die from scourging over the years, and so the Romans had perfected the art of inflicting just enough pain to ensure that a person suffered but didn't die immediately. In other words, they knew how to prolong suffering.

We read in **Matthew 27:26** that after Jesus had been scourged, He was handed over to be crucified. There would have been no dignity in it, as Jesus made His way to the place of His crucifixion. Beaten and bloody, surrounded by jeering crowds on all sides. Poor Mary being made to watch Him suffer. A crown of thorns had been rammed onto His head, causing even more pain and torment.

And as He arrived at Calvary, He was thrown on top of a wooden stake and six-inch nails were driven into His hands. The pain of that would have shot through His bloodied body. The feet come next, the pain doubtless excruciating. Any slight movement now would have caused untold agony for Jesus. As the cross is lifted up and planted into the ground, the trauma of that would have sent shockwaves through His battered body.

The weight of His body, and the terrible blood loss, would have caused His body to sag. This, in turn, would have torn at His hands. As He moved to take the pressure off His hands He would have piled more pressure on His feet. The nails now tear through the muscles in His feet. Inevitably, He tires and begins to sag again. Now there is pressure in His chest and lungs. It's hard to breathe. But there is nothing He can do to ease His pain and His suffering. Any movement now means unspeakable agony.

After three hours of this the Bible records that Jesus breathed His last.

Now, at this point in the story we could be forgiven for feeling sorry for Jesus. For the injustice of an innocent man having to go through all of that. If this were the end of the story then, yes, it would be sad, but it wouldn't be unique. It wouldn't be special. After all, many men and women have been unlawfully killed over the years. Many innocent people have gone to their deaths. Many of them have been tortured and murdered just as horrifically. They've been starved to death, boiled to death, fed to wild animals, beheaded, used as human candles, burned to death. All for the crime of being Christians. In fact, the soil of our planet is drenched in the blood of Christian martyrs through the ages.

But there was something different about this death. Something remarkable.

Jesus *volunteered to die* in this cruel, barbaric way.

VOLUNTARY SUFFERING

Very rarely will anyone die for a righteous person, though
for a good person someone might possibly dare to die.
(Romans 5:7)

The incredible thing about Jesus is that *He went willingly
to His death*. He *allowed Himself* to be taken when
Roman soldiers and an angry mob of religious leaders
found Him in the Garden of Gethsemane on the night
of His arrest. He *allowed Himself* to be put on trial – even
though He and the Jewish leaders knew it was illegal (the
Jews couldn't try people at night or in secret). He didn't
speak a word in His own defence as He stood in front of
Pilate, the Roman governor at the time.

Time and again in the New Testament we read of Jesus
warning His disciples that He had come to die. Three times He
tells them so in **John 10:11-17**:

> *I am the good shepherd. The good shepherd lays down his life
> for the sheep.* **(John 10:11)**

Just as the Father knows me and I know the Father – and I lay down my life for the sheep. (**John 10:15**)

The reason my Father loves me is that I lay down my life – only to take it up again. (**John 10:17**)

Then comes the real clincher in **John 10:18**: *'No one takes it from me, but I lay it down of my own accord. I have authority to lay it down and authority to take it up again. This command I received from my Father.'* Notice there what Jesus is saying:

Nobody takes my life from me.

What Jesus did on the cross, He did willingly. *He knew* what was coming. *He knew* there would be pain, suffering and humiliation – and incredibly, *He willingly embraced it.*

We live in a society where there is a lot of confusion about Jesus – about who He was and what He did. Many people think that He was probably a good man. Nothing more than a Jewish rabbi who went around teaching people to love one another and be kind to puppies. A man, ultimately, caught and tried by Roman courts and sentenced to death for His crimes. A man, probably outside of His time, who was dragged to His death and who accidentally kick-started a worldwide religion.

But is this what the Bible teaches? That Jesus was a man of the people? That He started a movement against the oppressive Roman rulers but was caught and killed before His time?

One of the great things about the Bible is that it is like a personal time machine. We can travel back in time to almost any point in the history of Jesus' ministry to observe what was going on. So, let's travel back in time to **John 18** to take a look for ourselves at how Jesus spent His last hours on earth. Was He really frightened? Was He really out of control and in despair?

John 18:1-11 records the finals hours leading up to His death for us:

> When he had finished praying, Jesus left with his disciples and crossed the Kidron Valley. On the other side there was a garden, and he and his disciples went into it. Now Judas, who betrayed him, knew the place, because Jesus had often met there with his disciples. So Judas came to the garden, guiding a detachment of soldiers and some officials from the chief priests and the Pharisees. They were carrying torches, lanterns and weapons. Jesus, knowing all that was going to happen to him, went out and asked them, 'Who is it you want?' 'Jesus of Nazareth,' they replied. 'I am he,' Jesus said. (And Judas the traitor was standing there with them.) When Jesus said, 'I am he,' they drew back and fell to the ground. Again he asked them, 'Who is it you want?'
>
> 'Jesus of Nazareth,' they said. Jesus answered, 'I told you that I am he. If you are looking for me, then let these men go.' This happened so that the words he had spoken would be fulfilled: 'I have not lost one of those you gave me.' Then Simon Peter, who had a sword, drew it and struck the high priest's servant, cutting off his right ear. (The servant's name was Malchus.) Jesus commanded Peter, 'Put your sword away! Shall I not drink the cup the Father has given me?'

To understand what is happening here, we need to understand some of the details that led Jesus up to this point. Because, at first reading, it appears that Jesus has been cornered in Gethsemane and has nowhere to run. But looks can be deceiving, as we shall go on to see.

The phrase 'his hour' is very important in the book of John. We read the phrase for the first time in **John 2:4**. 'Woman, why do you involve me?' Jesus replied. 'My hour has not yet come.' At that point He was talking to Mary before He performed His first miracle at a wedding. We read the phrase again when Jewish leaders try to arrest Him in **John 7:30**: 'At this they tried to seize him, but no one laid a hand on him, because his hour had not yet come.' Again, we hear the phrase used in **John 8:20** when an argument breaks out about whether Jesus is lying to the people concerning His deity. 'He spoke these words while teaching in the temple courts near the place where the offerings were put. Yet no one seized him, because his hour had not yet come.'

Then, as He enters into the last week of His life, the tone changes. In **John 12:23** we read, 'Jesus replied, "**The hour has come** for the Son of Man to be glorified."' Later on in the same chapter, as He thinks about the horror that is to come, we read this in **John 12:27**: 'Now my soul is troubled, and what shall I say? "Father, save me from this hour"? No, it was for this very reason **I came to this hour**.' Again, in **John 13:1,** 'It was just before the Passover Festival. Jesus knew that **the hour had come** for him to leave this world and go to the Father.' Just before His arrest in **John 18** we read the phrase again as He prays to God the Father in **John 17:1**. 'After Jesus said this, he looked toward heaven and prayed: "Father, **the hour has come.** Glorify your Son, that your Son may glorify you."'

There is no doubt from the Bible that as Jesus was arrested and put on trial, He knew that His hour had come. But, what exactly was this hour He was constantly referring to, and that had now suddenly come upon Him?

Simply this.

The hour of His death was coming and Jesus knew it. He knew that if the devil was to be defeated and the curse of sin was to be reversed, then He had to go to the cross. He had to experience the extreme suffering that was about to come His way. Therefore, as we enter into **John 18,** it's important we grasp that *Jesus was fully aware that the time for His death was almost upon Him.* He wasn't dragged kicking and screaming to the cross. On the contrary, in his darkest hour He doesn't hide away, or attempt to make a run for it. He goes to His normal hangout joint in the Garden of Gethsemane. How do you think Judas found Him? There was no CCTV or satellite imagery to pinpoint His location. In His last hours Jesus goes to His normal teaching spot. It is vital we don't miss this important detail.

When I was a young man on the run from the law, there were certain rules that I followed in order to keep from being caught. Number one was to *never* go to my regular hangout joints. That was the first place the police would look for me. Jesus was smart. I mean, He'd avoided capture up until this point, right? So, why did He break the golden rule and go to His usual hangout joint?

> **Because John wants us to understand that Jesus knew His hour had come and He was fully prepared to face it.**

Consequently, as Judas enters the scene stage left, it doesn't come as a shock to Jesus. He doesn't see him leading the mob up the garden and put His hands over His mouth in horror and surprise. The other disciples may have. We don't know because we are not told, but I suspect they would have been raging at this betrayal by Judas. This is a man who had been with them over the past three years, after all. They'd lived and laughed and broken bread together. Of course, they would have been angry and shocked. But not Jesus. He knew His hour had come and He even knew who His betrayer would be. He knew all the way back in **John 6:70-71** when He told the disciples clearly. *"'Have I not chosen you, the Twelve? Yet* one of you is a devil!" (He meant Judas, the son of Simon Iscariot, who, though one of the Twelve, was later to betray him.)'

In the moment of His arrest at Gethsemane, the forces of evil thought they were coming to take Jesus against His will. But the reality was that what was about to occur in that Garden, in His sham trial in front of the Jewish religious leaders, in His being taken to Pontius Pilate, to the scourging, to the baying crowds, to the Roman soldiers that gambled for His clothes, all the way to the cross, is about to be done *by the willing consent of Jesus*.

The early church was clear about this. Listen to one of the first ever sermons, given after the death and resurrection of Jesus in **Acts 2:22-23 (ESV)**: *'Men of Israel, hear these words: Jesus of Nazareth, a man attested to you by God with mighty works and wonders and signs that God did through him in your midst, as you yourselves know –* **this Jesus, delivered up according to the definite plan and foreknowledge of God***, you crucified and killed by the hands of lawless men.'*

Jesus Christ wasn't another victim like us. He wasn't a helpless, powerless bystander as He was led to his cruel death to be flogged, beaten, mocked, and humiliated. On the contrary, He came for *this hour*. Everything Jesus does He does willingly out of loving obedience, in order to glorify the Father in heaven.

In considering Jesus, just think about all that pain and humiliation He was about to go through. The false arrest. The jealous religious leaders, the crooked and cowardly Roman governor, the malicious Roman soldiers, and the jeering crowds. Think about His bloody body, mercilessly ripped open, a crown of thorns rammed onto His head, nails cruelly hammered in to His soft flesh, the agony and terror of slowly suffocating to death.

He knew it was all coming. And He embraced it all.

Yet, if only this was the extent of His suffering.

But it wasn't.

Not by a long shot.

Because Jesus steps forward in the garden and says these awful, terrifying words.

Shall I not drink the cup the Father has given me?
(Jesus)

JESUS & THE CUP OF GOD'S WRATH

'*I must drink this cup the Father has given me.*'

What a strange thing for Jesus to say. What does He mean by this?

Well, in the Bible, *the cup* is deeply connected to God's judgement against sinners. It is connected to Christ's suffering. It represents God's awful, final justice against sinners. It speaks to the full, holy, terrifying, settled wrath of God raining down on the unrepentant.

Let's understand that the wrath of God is not like the wrath of a scorned lover, or a drunken wife-beater. It is not borne out of spite or malice. It is His settled opposition to all that is evil in the world.

In **Psalm 75:7-8 (ESV)** it says, '*But it is God who executes judgment, putting down one and lifting up another. For in the hand of the Lord there is a cup with foaming wine, well mixed, and he pours out from it, and all the wicked of the earth shall drain it down to the dregs.*'

In **Isaiah 51:17 (ESV)** it says, 'Wake yourself, wake yourself, stand up, O Jerusalem, you who have drunk from the hand of the LORD the cup of his wrath, who have drunk to the dregs the bowl, the cup of staggering.'

In **Jeremiah 25:15-17 (ESV)** it says, 'Thus the LORD, the God of Israel, said to me: 'Take from my hand this cup of the wine of wrath, and make all the nations to whom I send you drink it. They shall drink and stagger and be crazed because of the sword that I am sending among them.' So I took the cup from the LORD's hand, and made all the nations to whom the LORD sent me drink it.'

In **Matthew 20:22** Jesus asked His disciples if they thought that they were ready to drink from the cup that He was to drink. 'We can,' they foolishly answered. They had no understanding of what Jesus was saying. They couldn't have, otherwise they would never had agreed to it. Jesus knew what terrors this meant: To have the full wrath of Almighty God come bearing down upon Him. That's why He prays in **Matthew 26:39 (ESV)**, 'My Father, if it be possible, let this cup pass from me; nevertheless, not as I will, but as you will.'

They didn't know it at the time, but the disciples would go on to drink from their own cup of suffering. But it would be nothing compared to that which Jesus was about to drink.

Jesus was about to face the full, settled fury of God's anger against all the rebellious sins in the world.

All the injustice, all of the evil, all of the abuse, the killing, the rape, the incest, the paedophilia, the neglect, the self-righteousness, the pride, the arrogance, the greed, the pain and the suffering. All God's righteous, settled anger would be brought down to bear upon His sinless Son. In that moment, in that garden in Gethsemane, *Jesus knew*.

He must drink this cup, He tells us, for His Father had given it to Him. But wait. *That can't be right, can it? The Father has given it to Him? The Father planned all this out? To watch His beloved Son being beaten, abused, jeered, crucified and then to top it all, to turn His full anger against Him? How is that fair? How is that right? How is that just? How is that not cruel abuse? A so-called loving Father allowing that to happen to His innocent son. Punishing Him for crimes He did not commit.*

How can we believe in a God like that?

SAO LUIS, NORTHERN BRAZIL, 2003

My wife, Miriam, calls me into our youngest daughter's bedroom. 'There's something wrong, Mez. She doesn't look right.' I peer into the cot and Lydia, not yet two years old, is lying there, limp and lifeless. She's been ill for the past 24 hours. I pick her up, trying not to show the panic I feel inside. 'Maybe we should take her to the hospital,' I suggest. 'Get the car, love.' Miriam runs to get the car, as I wrap her pale little body into a blanket.

She drives as I sit in the back with Lydia cradled in my arms. She has lost a serious amount of body weight. She can't drink or eat and when she speaks her words come out as half-whispered croaks. We drive as fast as we can to the nearest hospital, but there's a problem. We've only been in Brazil for a couple of months and we don't speak the language. Regardless, I rush into the reception and hold my child up and ask for help. 'Doente,' I say. The Brazilian word for sick. The bemused lady behind the counter points us over to the waiting area. 'Doente!' I say, more forcefully this time. Still, she shoos us away to the waiting area and jabbers something indiscernible at me.

We sit down. As we look around the full horror of where we are hits us. We've been so busy rushing in and trying to communicate to the receptionist that we haven't really taken in our surroundings. The place is packed. People are sitting or lying on the ground everywhere. The temperature is in the high 90s and the stench of human sweat, blood, sickness and death is incredible. Next to us an old man dies where he lies. A nurse comes past and just puts a sheet over the body. No words are spoken. She didn't even stop to check his pulse. A new horror dawns on me.

What have I brought my child to?

Soon, we are ushered into another waiting area, this time for children. We walk into a small side room and several other sick children are lying on beds surrounded by concerned family members. There is blood on the floor and faeces on the wall.

It is a brutal scene.

A man in a white uniform enters and starts trying to find a vein to get some fluid into her little body. But she is so dehydrated, he can't find one. Time and again he jabs his needle into her and she croaks in pain as he vainly tries to attach her to a saline drip. After about half-a-dozen attempts at this I grab his arm and firmly say, 'No!' He goes away as my wife and I scramble for tissues to wipe her bleeding arms.

Some time later, an older man comes in and explains to us in broken English that if we do not get some fluid into her, then Lydia will die. The only way we can do it, he informs us, is to go through the soles of her feet. 'It is going to hurt her,' he tells us. We quickly agree, and so he instructs me to place my body weight across her chest to stop her struggling as my wife holds her pale little legs.

She cries and screams and pleads with me through tearstained eyes to make the man stop hurting her. She is in agony and I am allowing *it to happen to her. It is the most traumatic experience of my life. Watching my baby suffer and feeling responsible for making it worse. But I know that if I don't do this, then she will die.*

I choke back my tears and try to comfort her as best I can. I know it's terrible, but I am more scared of what will happen to her if we don't put her through this.

I think about this story often, as I consider the wrath of God being poured out upon Jesus. Imagine if, as a stranger to my family, you'd walked into that hospital room all those years ago and saw me holding down a defenceless two-year-old child, who was begging me to stop hurting her. What would you instinctively think? At first glance you would probably be horrified – scandalised even. You would wonder what was going on. It might even appear that I, as her father, was both cruel and unloving.

And yet, would your emotional response be different if you were aware of all the facts leading up to that moment? If you could see and understand the bigger picture? I think it would. I think you would come to realise that I had to do what I did, not because I hated my child and wanted her to suffer, but because I loved my child with every fibre of my being and wanted her to live. I acted in the way I did because I could see the bigger picture that her two-year-old mind could not begin to comprehend. She didn't realise that without this intervention, cruel and painful as it was, she would surely die. Yes, in that moment the cure was terrible, awful in every way imaginable, but it was nothing to what awaited her had I not permitted it.

In the same way, many people do not like the thought of God the Father allowing His innocent Son to suffer the full torment of His wrath in the place of guilty sinners. Some even liken it to a form of cosmic child abuse. But that is because they do not comprehend the full picture of why this voluntary sacrifice was necessary. In that moment in Gethsemane, Jesus knew what nobody else there did. He knew that the storm of God's wrath was coming. That's why He prayed the way He did in **Luke 22:42**: *'Father, if you are willing, take this cup from me; yet not my will, but yours be done.'*

We have no real comprehension of the horror that went on as Jesus the man suffered the most intense sense of agony and isolation ever known. Yet, Jesus the God-Man walked toward all of it with His head held high and a focused determination in His heart to face the unspeakable horrors of what was coming.

John 19:30 NASB records these words. *'Therefore when Jesus had received the sour wine, He said, "It is finished!" And He bowed His head and gave up His spirit.'* As He cried out, He was reciting **Psalm 22** to the assembled crowd.

He felt like the Father has deserted Him, forsaken Him, abandoned Him.

As a man, He felt that true pain of separation. He felt the deep loss of that perfect communion.

In His death, as God's wrath was poured out on Him, God, in effect, laid the sins *of the whole world* upon His shoulders. We read in **1 Corinthians 5:21** that *He who knew no sin was made sin.*

> **To be clear, at no time did Jesus sin. He bore our sins.**

> *The pain.*
> *The humiliation.*
> *The fear.*
> *The flogging.*
> *The cross.*
> *The wrath.*

Some of us know the horror and injustice of being falsely accused of crimes we didn't commit. Imagine the perfect God-Man voluntarily bearing the shame and sin of all the world upon His bloody shoulders. He had done no wrong, yet He took our wrongs upon Himself.

> He was cursed like a common criminal.
> Like a child abuser.
> Like a rapist.
> He was cursed like a heroin addict.
> Like a burglar.
> Like a greedy businessman.
> Like an arrogant doctor.
> Like a vicious gossip.

For people like you and me.

This leads us to one of the most important questions we could ever ask.

WHY?

He is despised and rejected by men,
A Man of sorrows and acquainted with grief.
And we hid, as it were, our faces from Him;
He was despised, and we did not esteem Him.

Surely He has borne our griefs
And carried our sorrows;
Yet we esteemed Him stricken,
Smitten by God, and afflicted.

But He was wounded for **our transgressions**,
He was bruised for **our iniquities;**
The chastisement for our peace was upon Him,
And by His stripes we are healed.

All we like sheep have gone astray;
We have turned, every one, to his own way;
And the Lord has laid on Him the iniquity of us all.

He was oppressed and He was afflicted,
Yet He opened not His mouth;
He was led as a lamb to the slaughter,

And as a sheep before its shearers is silent,
So He opened not His mouth.

He was taken from prison and from judgment,
And who will declare His generation?
For He was cut off from the land of the living;
For the transgressions of My people He was stricken.

And they made His grave with the wicked –
But with the rich at His death,
Because He had done no violence,
Nor was any deceit in His mouth.

Yet it pleased the LORD to bruise Him;
He has put Him to grief.
(Isaiah 53:3-10a, NKJV)

HALIFAX, WEST YORKSHIRE, 1989

We'd been working as a team for months. Sometimes we'd go to the next city and split up. Each of us had anywhere between 5–10 different credit cards. The key was to spend small amounts in many different places. Supermarkets were the best. Then dump the card and move on to the next one.

Other times we'd cause a disturbance in a shop or market, and then one or two of us would steal whatever we could while the owner was distracted.

We never get caught. We are too quick and too clever to make that mistake. Money piles in. Drugs pile high. Life is great. Doing what we want, when we want, how we want, and to whom we want.

Nobody can stop us.

HALIFAX, WEST YORKSHIRE, 1990

I hear the shouts first, then the sound of a door being smashed in. Before I know it, the lights are on in my room, temporarily blinding me, and a horde of police officers bursts through the door. I don't have time to think or to panic or to react. I just sit there in my boxer shorts, confused at first, and then resigned to what is going on. It's a raid. Our little spree is over. We're well and truly busted. Stolen goods lie all around the flat. Drugs and cash on a table nearby.

A big, burly policeman pulls me to my feet. 'Off we go, son. Time to pay for what you've done.'

CONSEQUENCES

For we must all appear before the judgment seat of Christ, so that each of us may receive what is due us for the things done while in the body, whether good or bad.
(2 Corinthians 5:10)

When Adam & Eve first rebelled against God they opened up a world of trouble. Not only for themselves, but for the whole of the human race that would follow. Adam and Eve couldn't have known what would happen the day they made that fateful decision to listen to the devil, and to go against God's command not to eat the forbidden fruit. It probably seemed like a little thing to them at the time. A piece of fruit hanging off a tree. I mean, how much of a big deal could it be? Yet, tragically for them, and for us, that one little choice opened the floodgates to disaster and suffering on a terrifyingly global scale.

There were consequences to their sin. There are consequences to ours.

Serious consequences.

The wages of sin is death. (**Romans 6:23**)

Jesus knew that God could not let the sin of Adam and Eve go unpunished. They were warned in **Genesis 2:17** what would happen if they disobeyed God. *'You will surely die,'* He said. As we know, from the moment they sinned, their relationship with God and to one another changed. But, so did their relationship to creation. The ground was now cursed instead of blessed. The woman would now endure the pain of childbirth and the man would have to toil in order to get food from the ground. The moment they ate the forbidden fruit, their bodies began to die, and soon the glories of Eden would fade into the mists of time as they were banished from the presence of God.

Spiritually, before the Lord, they were both now dead, separated from Him. They could no longer be in His presence. Although it took them many, many years to die physically, death was now in motion and it would affect the entire world. This is how the Apostle Paul explained it to the church in **Romans 5:12.** *'Therefore, just as sin entered the world through one man, and death through sin, and in this way death came to all people, because all sinned...'*

In fact, it doesn't take long for sin to spread its poison, and in **Genesis 4** we read the account of how Cain killed his brother Abel in a fit of jealousy. Murder had entered the world. Really that should have been that. God should have left us to our own devices. Just pulled back and let us destroy ourselves.

But, *God so loved the world.*

So much so that He made a way for people to make atonement for their sins. We read this in **Leviticus 17:11**: *'For the life of a creature is in the blood, and I have given it to you to make atonement* for yourselves on the altar; it is the blood that makes atonement for one's life.'

Atonement is another word for cleansing. It means to remove sin. In the Old Testament, God's people made an animal sacrifice to atone for their sins.

The consequence for our sin is *spiritual* and *physical death*.

Isaiah 59:2 is clear about this: '*But your iniquities have separated you from your God; your sins have hidden his face from you, so that he will not hear.*'

The terrible truth is that because we are sinners, rebels, before Him, He will not listen to our prayers or cries for help. Jesus knew this terrible truth. That is why He went to such extreme ends.

Jesus did not die on the cross to make us feel better about ourselves. He didn't do it to lift our self-esteem. He did it to save us from the eternal wrath of God being poured out on us in hell.

He did it to fulfil all the Father's righteousness.

But, when Christ appeared as a high priest of the good things to come, He entered through the greater and more perfect tabernacle, not made with hands, that is to say, not of this creation; and not through the blood of goats and calves, but through His own blood, He entered the holy place once for all, having obtained eternal redemption. For if the blood of goats and bulls and the ashes of a heifer sprinkling those who have been defiled, sanctify for the cleansing of the flesh, how much more will the blood of Christ, who through the eternal Spirit offered Himself without blemish to God, cleanse your conscience from dead works to serve the living God?
(Hebrews 9:11-14 NASB)

Jesus took the full consequences of our sin: God's wrath poured down upon us and eternal suffering and separation from Him in hell.

All this so that *we do not have to face the terrors that He did.*

> That's why He came to earth. That's why He went voluntarily to His death.

In the Old Testament, in order to illustrate to the people of Israel the seriousness of their sin problem, God instituted the sacrificial system. **Leviticus 16** lays out the rules on how the priests were to approach God on behalf of the people. We read this in **Leviticus 16:6-10**:

> *Aaron is to offer the bull for his own sin offering to make atonement for himself and his household. Then he is to take the two goats and present them before the LORD at the entrance to the tent of meeting. He is to cast lots for the two goats – one lot for the LORD and the other for the scapegoat. Aaron shall bring the goat whose lot falls to the LORD and sacrifice it for a sin offering. But the goat chosen by lot as the scapegoat shall be presented alive before the LORD to be used for making atonement by sending it into the wilderness as a scapegoat.*

So, the point of the first sacrifice was to act like a visual aid to the people, as the blood shed cleansed the people of their sins. These sacrifices ultimately pointed people to Jesus, who shed His blood on the cross to make atonement for the sins of His people.

The second sacrifice, the scapegoat, was sent away into the wilderness as a sign that the people's sins were carried off to a remote place. There, the scapegoat would wander alone, cut off from God and His people. This, too, pointed people to Jesus, who bore our sins on the cross and suffered and died alone.

Now, the problem with all this is that sacrificing goats and bulls and lambs didn't fully solve the problem of our sin.

God's people still sinned.

We still sin.

So, these sacrifices had to go on day after day, week after week, month after month, year after year. An endless procession of bloody sacrifices. In **Hebrews 10:1** the author tells us that the sacrifices didn't *'make perfect those who draw near to worship'*. In fact, He says in **Hebrews 10:4**: *'It is impossible for the blood of bulls and goats to take away sins.'*

Of course, the sacrificial system was only ever meant to be temporary. It was only there to point us to Jesus. The Old Testament saints waited in faith-fuelled hope for that glorious day when Jesus would come to earth to deal with the problem *once and for all.* **Hebrews 10:11-12** goes on to explain. *'Day after day every priest stands and performs his religious duties; again and again he offers the same sacrifices, which can never take away sins. But when this priest (Jesus) had offered for all time one sacrifice for sins, he sat down at the right hand of God.'*

Did you notice that? On the cross, Jesus offered *a once-for-all-time sacrifice for sins*. No need for all those animal sacrifices anymore. No need for all that bloodshed. Why? Because by taking upon himself the full wrath of God, **Jesus was the full and final sacrifice**.

Forever.

That's why, when Jesus came, John the Baptist said this about Him in **John 1:29**: *'Behold, the lamb of God who takes away the sins of the* *world.'* That's why Jesus tells His disciples in **Matthew 26:28** that His blood would be *'poured out for many for the forgiveness of sins'.*

What's even more incredible is that He did this *while we were still sinners.* In other words, He did it even though we were guilty, ungrateful rebels; enemies who cursed His name and refused to live according to His commands. Listen, again to the Apostle Paul, teaching the church in **Romans 5:8**: *'But God demonstrates his own love for us in this: While we were still sinners, Christ died for us.'*

Jesus came because sin had consequences. Deadly, physical, eternal ones.

Yet, there is still more to consider.

Incredibly, there is something far worse in this world than the pain of our abuse.

There is something far more terrifying than the fear of our earthly tormentors.

> For we must all appear before the judgment seat of Christ, so that each of us may receive what is due us for the things done while in the body, whether good or bad. **(2 Corinthians 5:10)**

If only physical death were our biggest problem.

JUDGEMENT

People are destined to die once, and after that to face judgment.
(Hebrews 9:27)

The truly scary thing about death is that it is not the worst thing that can happen to us.

It is what happens *after* death that should most concern us. Because the Bible teaches that *every single human being* that has ever lived, and will ever live, will have to *stand before Him one day in judgement*.

Every single one of us will have to give an account to our creator for how we spent our lives.

Despite what we've been led to believe, death is not the end. Far from it. In fact, it is just the beginning. Death is the doorway through which we will step into eternity. When we've breathed our last on earth we will step into the spiritual reality of the next life.

King Solomon, looking back on his life, wrote a book in the Bible called Ecclesiastes. In **Ecclesiastes 12:14** he had this to say about God's final judgement: *'For God will bring every deed into judgment, including every hidden thing, whether it is good or evil.'*

Did you notice what he says here? *Every hidden thing, good or evil will be brought into the light.* Who we have really been will be laid bare. What we've really thought will come to light. All the little things we think we have gotten away with over the years will have to be accounted for.

On the one hand this gives me great comfort. To know that my abusers, who got away with so much, will one day give an account to Almighty God. Then they'll be made to pay for their crimes against me. Their shame will on display for all to see.

They will suffer. And it will be glorious.

On the other hand, I fear this news. I fear it because I know what I am like inside. My secret, shameful thoughts. My sins. I may have done jail time for the crimes I committed, but I can assure you that I didn't get caught for every one of them.

Not even close.

Here's the awful reality: I, too, will stand before Almighty God in the judgement. All my sin will be laid bare before Him. And I may not have harmed children or abused my wife, but I have been a rebel against God nonetheless.

I will be judged guilty, regardless of my upbringing. Regardless of my childhood traumas. Regardless of the pain and chaos of my life. I will be found wanting in the final judgement. I will be found guilty of ignoring God, of taking His name in vain, of denying His very existence. I have been a rebel and I will have to account for it.

And it will be terrifying.

The horror we feel when we turn on the news and we see a small child has been raped and murdered. The cry for justice that goes up in our souls.

The rage that eats away at us at the thought of our abusers getting away with it.

The murderous thoughts of vengeance when we see somebody in the street that reminds us of our tormentors.

That does not even compare to the righteous hatred and anger God feels against sin and sinner.

ARMLEY PRISON, LEEDS, 1993

'Are you sure it's him?'
'It's him.'

There wasn't much of him to look at. Average height. Average weight. Scrawny-looking, really. He had that haunted look in his eyes. That furtive, guilty look, like he was scared somebody would find out who he really was and what he was doing time for.

Well, we had found out.

I piled the mashed potatoes onto his plate as he came by the server. He kept his head down, avoided any eye contact, and just kept on walking. 'Pervert,' whispered the convict next to him. 'Filthy beast!' spat another. The man kept walking, safe in the knowledge that he was protected by at least six prison wardens watching our every move.

'Who is he?' we asked our friend when we got back to the kitchens. 'What did he do?' 'He's a priest,' said my friend. 'No way!' I replied. 'He is.' 'How do you know that?' 'Because the animal married me and christened my children. That's how. He's in for sexually abusing some young lads. He got 18 months.' '18 months! I got more than that for possession of cannabis,' said one of our friends. We all fell silent,

thinking about what we'd heard. 'How do we get to him?' 'We can't. He's on protection. We'll never get to him.' 'True. But his food isn't on protection, is it?'

And so we spiked his food with spit, broken glass, dead cockroaches, anything we could lay our hands on. We had no idea whether he would eat it, but we didn't care. We just felt like we had to deliver justice in a system we felt had let him off too lightly. That's how it went in prison. The courts sentenced you, but the inmates dished out the justice. We decided who deserved a little bit more than the time they were given.

Prison justice we called it.

Real justice.

And we were more than happy to pass judgement on those we felt deserved it.

JESUS & JUSTICE

God is not only supremely merciful, but also supremely just. This justice requires (as God has revealed in the Word) that the sins we have committed against his infinite majesty be punished with both temporal and eternal punishments, of soul as well as body. We cannot escape these punishments unless satisfaction is given to God's justice.

(2.1). Thirty-Nine Articles of Faith

The Bible teaches that no person on earth is without sin. We read in **Ecclesiastes 7:20 NKJV**, *'For there is not a just man on earth who does good and does not sin.'* The Apostle Paul says something similar in **Romans 3:23**, reminding us that, *'All have sinned and fall short of the glory of God.'* In fact, God's assessment of the nature of the human race is pretty bleak:

> *'There is no one righteous, not even one; there is no one who understands; there is no one who seeks God. All have turned away, they have together become worthless; there is no one*

who does good, not even one.' 'Their throats are open graves; their tongues practice deceit.' 'The poison of vipers is on their lips.' 'Their mouths are full of cursing and bitterness.' 'Their feet are swift to shed blood; ruin and misery mark their ways, and the way of peace they do not know.' 'There is no fear of God before their eyes.' **(Romans 3:10-18)**

Understanding this, why do so many of us find it hard to believe that God wants justice? That He demands justice for the sins of the world? Why shouldn't God seek justice against the sin and rebellion of those He has lovingly created? Think of the almost-primal urge each of us has for justice when we have been sinned against, or when an innocent is hurt. Magnify that billions of times around the globe as God is faced with sin and rebellion in all its evil, God-denying shapes and sizes.

Why wouldn't He want justice?

In fact, He wouldn't be much of a God if He didn't.

Personally, I would have done anything – *anything at all* – to have brought my chief tormentor to justice before she died. To hear her crimes being read out for all to hear. To watch her reaction as a judge passed sentence. But I never pursued her. I never called the police and reported her, even though I had ample opportunity over the years.

I really don't know why I didn't.

Shame? Possibly. Guilt? Maybe. Embarrassment at allowing myself to be treated like that? Yes. Fear? Definitely. As the years went by, who she was and what she did just faded into the distance, to the point where I hardly ever thought about her. As for the others, I can barely remember their faces. There were so many homes and names and faces that it is all just one dense fog.

When I see a news report come on of a celebrity being accused or of children being abused and neglected, I follow it avidly, hoping that they get their just desserts. Because that's what really lies at the heart of our need for justice, isn't it? People getting what they deserve. So, of course a rapist deserves harsher justice than, say, a common burglar. That's how any normal human being would calculate justice.

In the Old Testament justice was *'an eye for any eye.'* This is how the prophet Obadiah explained it in **Obadiah 1:15**: *'The day of the LORD is near for all nations. As you have done, it will be done to you; your deeds will return upon your own head.'* In biblical terms, though, justice was always about getting what you deserved, **and no more**.

In fact, God was so concerned that people treat criminals fairly that six cities were set aside in Israel. These places were known as *cities of refuge*. They were there to protect people who'd committed crimes against others who might overreact in seeking justice. In the Old Testament the punishment for murder was death. But what about those who killed somebody unintentionally? How could they be protected from vengeful family members who would want an eye for an eye? Well, they could run to these cities and be assured of a fair trial.

In other words, in Bible times, God made sure that *justice operated within limits.*

If a man stole an apple, for example, justice would not be for that man to have his arm chopped off. Justice should be proportional to the crime committed. That's why so many of us get angry when abusers, particularly, often get off with what we see as *light* sentences. We feel they should get more. Instead of an eye for an eye, it often feels like a fingernail for an eye. If anything, we feel, because of the seriousness of the crimes, it should be more like a head for an eye. Yet, very often, it doesn't happen. We rarely see justice like this.

At least, not in the way that we would like.

Now, some people think that God is a bit more lenient in the New Testament. That He leaves all that eye for an eye stuff behind and ushers in a new era of love and forgiveness. Well, that's not strictly true. The God of the Old Testament is the God of the New Testament. He shows the same capacity for love, mercy and justice throughout the whole Bible. His standards do not change. He still demands perfect obedience from His people.

He is still the God of justice. Because God is good and just, the Supreme Judge of the universe, He must punish the crimes committed against Him. If He overlooked our crimes as if they'd never happened, or merely accepted an apology from us on the day of judgement and let us go free from his holy courtroom, then He would be corrupt and unjust. It is precisely because of His goodness that our sin must be punished, and it is why we deserve His justice and death sentence to eternal hell.

But there is more to God than that.

RIGHTEOUSNESS

There is no God apart from me, a righteous God and a
Saviour; there is none but me.

(Isaiah 45:21)

If, at the heart of the human race, there is a spirit of
lawless rebellion, then at the heart of Almighty God
lies *righteousness* and *justice*. The two go hand in hand. One
cannot exist without the other. God is so righteous that we,
in our present, sinful condition, cannot be in His presence.
When speaking to Moses in **Exodus 33:20** God says to him,
'You cannot see my face, for no one may see me and live.'

Listen to how the Apostle Paul describes God to Timothy, his
young student, in **1 Timothy 6:15b-16**. *'God, the blessed and only
Ruler, the King of kings and Lord of lords, who alone is immortal and
who lives in unapproachable light, whom **no one has seen or
can see**. To him be honour and might forever. Amen.'*

In effect, God is as unlike us as He could possibly be. Yes, we
have been victims of suffering. Yes, we have faced unthinkable
tragedies and crimes in our lives. Yes, life has been more than
unfair; cruel, even.

But none of that means we get a free pass on our sin.

God's justice *must* be served, and His righteousness *must* be upheld.

In short, because God is a God of *righteousness* and *justice*, His perfect, terrible judgement awaits every single one of us upon our deaths.

It soon became clear to me in the very early days of trying to understand Christianity that I only wanted justice on my terms and I certainly didn't want it for myself. I'd happily dish out judgement on those I think deserved it, but for myself and some close friends, I would be more inclined to mercy.

Yet, it was clear to me that the Bible taught that I was a sinner before a holy God. And what's more, I knew it. Strip back all of the anger, the pain, the shame, the guilt and the violent rage and I knew that I was a sinner. I knew that I was deserving of God's wrath. Of course, I'd suffered. But what a convenient excuse it was for me to live in open rebellion against my creator!

The more I learned about God, the more amazed I was by Him. I learned from **2 Peter 3:9** that God is long-suffering and wishes that all come to repentance. How thankful I was in my own life for this time I was given to repent of my sins!

Yet, His patience with me and the human race didn't mean that He would not serve justice. **Nahum 1:3** tells us, *'The Lord is slow to anger but great in power; the Lord will not leave the guilty unpunished.'* The wicked may think they are getting off, but their justice is only delayed for as long as God allows it.

God will only delay His justice for so long, and He will never, ever deny it.

Sooner or later the full wrath of God will be revealed from heaven *against all the ungodliness and unrighteousness of men (and women) who suppress the truth in unrighteousness.*

The death of Jesus demonstrates that justice has been served. God didn't just shrug off our sin as if it didn't matter.

Jesus, who was completely innocent, paid the full penalty that we deserved.

He bore the awful wrath of God when He gave his life on the cross, and in doing so God's righteousness was upheld.

All that waits for us upon our death is judgement.

Is there any hope for us?

YORKSHIRE, 1991

He is lying on the ground, bleeding heavily. A crowd of about 20 teenagers are shouting and swearing, egging me on. 'Smash him!' 'Don't let him get up.' I swing another boot and connect with his face. Blood spatters everywhere as his nose makes a loud popping sound. Even I am beginning to feel a bit ill at this point.

This is a lad who had beaten me senseless a couple of years before. He and a group of his friends had jumped me and battered me mercilessly with sticks and poles. At the time I had simply curled up into a ball and taken the beating silently. At that point in my life I was a pro in taking pain. That group had nothing on my stepmother.

Now, here we are, two years after she had gone from my life, and I don't lie down to take beatings anymore. I had memorised the lad's face, and when I see him walking into the local shop one day, I follow him and wait outside. 'Remember me?' I ask. He looks confused but not overly concerned. He's at least a foot taller than me and much heavier.

He doesn't see the milk bottle as I bring it down on his head. He just collapses to the floor and I pound on him, raining punch after punch into his prone body. I beat him until I run out of breath. Years of my pent-up frustration and anger at being a victim are unleashed on him. Well, I'm not one now and I won't be again.

'I'm sorry,' he sobs, his face covered in blood. 'Please. I'm sorry.' I bend down to take his hand and pull him to his feet. But, at the last second, I kick him in the face again. 'Stick your sorry!' I say at him through gritted teeth. 'You didn't stop beating me when you were with your mates. So why should I feel sorry for you?' My friends laugh and cheer.

I want justice. I need justice. This is me enforcing my brand of justice. It's unthinkable to show this lad mercy.

Even though I feel a twinge of guilt, I push it down. No mercy was shown to me and so I will show no mercy to him. Or anybody else who wants to hurt me, for that matter.

No mercy. Ever.

MERCY

Blessed are the merciful, for they will be shown mercy.
(Jesus)

Psalm **145:8-9** says, '*The* LORD *is gracious and compassionate, slow to anger and rich in love. The* LORD *is good to all; he has compassion on all he has made.*'

If justice is getting what we deserve, then mercy is *not getting what we deserve.* I had no time for mercy growing up, largely because I was shown none as a child. I was beaten, imprisoned, starved, abused and neglected for years. *I had done nothing to deserve it.* My tormentors were never brought to justice and they never showed a hint of mercy, even when I begged for it. Even when I was on my knees at five years old taking kicks to the kidneys. Even when I was starved for days on end, faint from the hunger, crying for help.

All I got was more abuse, more pain.

Yet, when I began to read the Bible I couldn't escape the fact that God is a merciful God. God is not like us, not even in the slightest. His creation rejects Him and rebels against His just rule. People do what they like and commit all sorts of evil acts. They laugh in the face of God. They deserve His justice. They deserve His holy wrath. Yet, what does He do? He doesn't sweep them away to their doom. Instead, He sends the Lord Jesus to earth. John writes in **1 John 4:10**, *'This is love: not that we loved God, but that he loved us and sent his Son as an atoning sacrifice for our sins.'*

I may have been a victim, but I know deep down that I was not guiltless. I had hurt people. I had lied. I had cheated. I had done terrible things. But, most grievous of all, I had denied my creator. I had cursed Him. I had shaken my fist at Him. I had blamed Him for my terrible life and all the bad decisions I had made.

Incredibly, He showed great patience with me. He loved me even when I hated Him. Still, His *righteousness* and *justice* demanded that I should pay the price for my sins. Yes, I would physically die. We all will. But, more than that, His justice demanded that I would face the full force of His holy wrath as He met me in judgement.

I used to tell myself that if God existed and I met Him, I would give Him a piece of my mind. I'd tell Him to 'stick heaven'. I told myself that I would prefer to go to hell with my friends anyway. After all, how much worse than this life could it be?

Of course, it was foolish thinking. Nor did I truly believe it. Usually I would be grandstanding for friends or high on some sort of narcotic. Often both. Deep down I was a mess, fighting hard to keep my sanity as my life spiralled out of control. I was aimless, hopeless, bitter, angry and lost.

So very, very lost.

I had no moral anchor or mooring to guide me through life. My whole identity was caught up in my childhood. I couldn't get past the pain. I couldn't get over the abuse. I couldn't let go of the neglect. Anger ate at me, day in and day out. Drugs did nothing to assuage me. Women did nothing to calm me. Prison stoked my rage further still.

I am so thankful that God is not like me. The Bible says that He is rich in mercy even though we deserve His justice and His wrath. It's important to understand that God does not show mercy at the expense of His justice. He doesn't just overlook our sins. He must punish them in order for His wrath to be satisfied and His justice to be upheld. So, in His mercy, He satisfied His justice by punishing Jesus on behalf of sinners.

> *Jesus took the punishment for the crimes I had committed.*

This led the way for his mercy to be offered to guilty sinners. Without the sacrifice of Jesus and the mercy of God we are lost.

> Lost for all eternity.
> Damned.
>
> God *must* punish sin.
> God *will* punish sin.
> He *has* to.

His punishment will, quite literally, be hell for us.

HELL ON EARTH?

'*Would you like one? Go on, take it.*' In her hands was a bar of chocolate. I wasn't sure what to do. Was it a trick? **She'd** never given me anything before. Except pain. '*Take it. You've been a good boy.*' The room fell quiet. All her friends were watching me. Some of them smiled encouragingly and so I stepped forward to take it. Quick as a flash, **she** punched me in the head and I fell to the ground. The whole room erupted in laughter. '*Get up!*' **she** ordered me. '*If you want it then you have to be quicker than that.*' '*I don't want it,*' I said, rising to my feet, my ears still ringing from the blow. '*Take it.*' Her eyes glinted, and I knew that look all too well. If I took it **she** would hit me and if I didn't, who knew what punishment **she** would inflict on me for embarrassing her in front of her friends? I stepped forward and, right on cue, **she** punched me in the stomach. I stumbled back winded, as the room broke out in raucous laughter.

Tears formed in my eyes. Why did **she** have to do this to me? I hadn't done anything to her. One of her friends took pity on me. '*Aw, leave him. He's had enough, the poor little mite. Give him the chocolate.*' '*He's getting nothing,*' **she** spat back, and her friend averted her eyes. **She** turned to me. 'Stop snivelling and get out of my sight.' I ran, gratefully, to my room. I sat there, relieved it was over, yet knowing that **she** would find some new way to torment and humiliate me tomorrow. And the day after that. And the day after that.

What kind of hell is this?

'Right, who wants chips?' The sound echoes throughout the house. 'Me!' comes the excited cry from all six children. Chips are a treat and often only happen if Dad had won at the bookies. 'Right, you. Off you go.' **She** points at me. 'Don't forget to get salt and vinegar.' I take the money from her hand. 'And you better be quick about it.' I rush to the end of our road and join the queue in the local fish & chips shop. The kind man behind the counter leans over to get my order and take my money. 'You're a brave lad coming out on your own, son,' he says kindly. 'How old are you, then, son?' 'Six,' I say proudly. He mutters something to himself and tells me to get straight home and no talking to strangers. I run home as fast as my little legs can carry me.

As soon as I get through the front door I am greeted by the others like a conquering hero. Chips for everybody! We'd be kings and queens for a night. Or so I thought. **She** comes up behind me, takes the parcels of food out of my hands and asks, 'What took you so long?' 'There was a big queue and I had to wait,' I reply. 'I think you're trying to be funny, taking all that time. Are you trying to be funny?' I don't understand the question. 'No,' I say. 'No chips for you,' **she** declares, as **she** shoves me back against the kitchen door. 'But that's not fair!' I cry.

Big mistake.

Before I could dodge, **she** had punched me in the head and thrown me by the hair across the kitchen floor. I lay there sobbing, more because I knew my chance at chips had gone, than for anything else. All the other children were watching me. Her own four were smirking, safe in the knowledge that they would eat chips, for they could do no wrong in her eyes. My sister was frozen in place at the kitchen table. Not daring to move. Not daring to breathe. I knew the battle that was going on inside her. She wanted to help me, but she also wanted chips. 'Shut your noise and get up!' **she** barked at me. I stood, shakily, not meeting her eyes for fear of angering her further still. A little piece of me still clung on to the hope that I could turn this around and get chips tonight. But, inevitably, **she** had other ideas.

'Stand there.' I stood, rooted to the spot, and watched as they opened their chips and poured them onto their plates. The smell was amazing. Heavenly. 'Don't look at him!' **she** ordered the others. 'Let's eat.' And so I stood there and watched them eat. **She** smiled and savoured each chip, looking me in the eye while she did so. Her children did the same. 'Wow!' they said, 'These are the best chips ever!' My sister ate silently with her head down. 'You!' **she** screamed at her. 'Tell him how good these chips are now. Or I'll take the lot off you.' 'Mmmm,' my sister said. 'They're absolutely amazing.' **She** made me stand there until they'd all finished eating. Then **she** made me clear the table and wash the plates. Then **she** sent me to my room without any food. To worry about what new terror **she** would inflict upon me tomorrow. I couldn't sleep. I daren't. I wondered how long **she** would make me go without food this time. I haven't eaten for two days.

What kind of hell is this?

ENGLAND, 1995

It was another good service at the church. I mean, I didn't understand a lot of it, but it was nice to be around Christians and it was nice to hear the Bible being explained. I'd only been going for a few weeks. I had recently become a Christian. I'd realised that I was a sinner in need of God's forgiveness and now my friends had brought me along to their church. It was great. I couldn't have been happier.

'Hello, Mez.' The minister shook my hand. 'How are you doing?' 'Cool, thanks,' I replied, desperate to get out for a smoke. An hour and a half without a smoke was a killer. 'Have you made a decision about Jesus yet?' he asked me. 'Oh yeah,' I said airily, 'I did that weeks ago. I'm team Jesus now, baby!' He looked at me, obviously slightly bemused. 'Well, praise the Lord! Tell me, how about your family and friends?' 'What about them?' I asked. 'What do they think of your new-found faith?' 'No idea, mate. I haven't spoken to them.' 'Well,' the minister leaned in, 'make sure you pray for them.' 'Don't you worry about that, mate. I pray for them every night. That they would burn in hell forever. Every single night without fail. That God would toast the lot of them. Well, not all of them. Just the ones who abused me the most.'

I was proud as punch. Here's me, being a Christian and praying and everything! But, the minister just looked horrified. 'Oh dear,' The minister said. 'Erm...I'm not sure that is a good idea.' 'Course it is,' I said. 'The Bible says the wicked will go to hell, right? Well, they're all wicked. So, they all get to go to hell. Excellent!'

THE GLORIOUS, WONDERFUL REALITY OF HELL

When I first came into contact with Christians, they mentioned hell to me. They talked about an eternity of pain, suffering and of torment. My response was, *'It didn't sound so different to my life growing up.'* I was a wreck, living on friends' floors, drugged out of my mind most days. *'And anyway,'* I said, warming to my theme, *'How do you know that this isn't hell we're living in now? It certainly feels a lot like what you're describing.'*

If we're honest, that's what most of us who have been through trauma feel, right? I mean, the threat of hell holds no fear for those of us who have lived through years of abuse and torment. Of course, my understanding of the Bible and the topic of hell grew as I studied it more and more. I read verses like **Matthew 22:13**, that describes hell as a place of *'darkness, where there will be weeping and gnashing of teeth'*. People would often describe it as a place of absolute loneliness, depression, despair and unrestrained, eternal evil.

Still, I would be unmoved. Again, it all sounded painfully familiar to me. And it probably does to you. What fear does eternal hopelessness hold when you feel eternally hopeless now? What fear does eternal torment hold when you are being horrifically, systematically, consistently and persistently abused almost every waking hour of every single day? When every waking minute is filled with the terror of wondering, *'What's coming next?'* When you hear the rattle of a door being opened and you freeze, wondering what mood they're going to be in. When they've had a bad day and now they're home to take it out on you. When nobody believes you and nobody hears your terrified screams and the smothered sounds of your sobs. When you're made to stand naked and exposed out of sheer, evil malice. When you're starved because, apparently, *'You don't deserve to eat.'*

Then, I discovered that Jesus talked about hell more than any other subject in the Bible. That pricked my ears up. Really? I thought Jesus just wandered around doing miracles and talking about love? I read **Matthew 13:41-42**: *'The Son of Man will send out his angels, and they will weed out of his kingdom everything that causes sin and all who do evil. They will throw them into the blazing furnace, where there will be weeping and gnashing of teeth.'* How brilliant did this sound, I thought?

It got better. **Mark 9:43a-48** was even more brutal: *'It is better for you to enter life maimed than with two hands to go into hell, where the fire never goes out. And if your foot causes you to stumble, cut it off. It is better for you to enter life crippled than to have two feet and be thrown into hell. And if your eye causes you to stumble, pluck it out. It is better for you to enter the kingdom of God with one eye than to have two eyes and be thrown into hell, where "the worms that eat them do not die, and the fire is not quenched."'* Imagine that! How glorious would that be? A place after death for all the rats who had terrorised, hurt, and abused me.

She would be there!

Forever!

I was so happy that I couldn't contain myself. I began to mention hell in my prayers. I would always sign off my time of prayer to God by asking Him to keep the fire extra hot for her and the rest of them that had tormented my sister and I for so long. It was such a release. Such a feeling of joy to be praying that way. It gave me a real sense of peace that God was going to burn all of them. For eternity. *'Lord,'* I remember praying, *'Send everybody,* **everybody***, there. To burn forever. To be tormented forever. And not just for those who abused me but for all the victims of abuse, Lord. Wherever they are. Send all those who deserve it straight to hell.'*

Hell was real. Brilliant. I absolutely loved it. I hoped the devil kept it extra hot for her and her sick friends.

THE TERRIBLE REALITY OF HEAVEN

ENGLAND, 1997

'*See that guy over there?' The pastor pointed to a thin-looking man in his late 20s, sitting nervously at the back of the hall. 'He just got out of prison. Go over and talk to him, Mez.' So, I wandered over and offered him my hand. 'Hey, what's happening?' I said. He eyed me nervously. 'Nothing much,' came the reply. 'Welcome to the church. Your first time here?' 'Yes,' he mumbled, nervously looking at the floor. 'I heard you just got out. Where were you?' He names the prison but it's not one I know. 'You a Christian?' I ask. 'Yeah,' he says. 'A couple of years now.' 'Good for you, mate. How long did you do?' I asked. 'I got six years,' came the reply. 'Yeah? Wow. Tough one. What for?' He suddenly turned pale. 'What do you mean?' 'I mean, what did you do jail for?' He knew what I meant. It was a standard question between jailbirds.*

I knew before he even opened his mouth that he was a sex offender. 'I was just stupid. I regret it now,' he said. 'Was it kids?' I asked him straight now, all pretence of being nice gone. He didn't answer. He just kept looking at his shoes. 'It was kids, wasn't it?' I hissed at him, worried that people would overhear. Still silence; looking at his shoes.

'You need to do one, mate,' I said. 'Now! Before I do something stupid.' He looked up and by now I was eyeball to eyeball with him. I smiled at a lady in the church, passing by with her three children. 'I better not see your face here again. Do you understand?' 'Yeah,' he whispered, and walked out the door just as the service was starting.

Afterwards, the pastor sought me out and asked me what had happened to the man. 'He scarpered, Pastor,' I said, feigning indifference. 'That's a shame,' replied the pastor, 'he seemed like a nice young man.' 'Well, he wasn't, Pastor. He was a sex offender. We are better off without him here. Simple as.'

The pastor stood staring at me for a couple of minutes, picking his words carefully. 'Look around, Mez. We are all sinners. Every single one of us. In God's sight we are all as terrible as sex offenders. God saves all kinds of people, Mez. Even the ones we don't particularly like.'

I was dumbstruck. No way did God save sex offenders. No way at all. But, I was too shocked to say anything. Later that same day, I became enraged by this thought. God saw me like a sex offender? What? That's not right. It couldn't be.

The church is for good people, I told myself. Well, if that's true, then why are you in church? came the instant reply in my mind. I'd been a Christian for two years and I hadn't ever thought about it. Does God save sex offenders? Does He let them into heaven?

No, He couldn't. Could He?

I came to realise pretty quickly that if there were people in the church that I thought shouldn't be there, then there would definitely be people in heaven that I thought shouldn't be there either. I liked the thought of heaven for myself and my loved ones. But for my abusers? My tormentors? No thanks.

Many people struggle with the thought of a loving God sending people to hell. Yet, these same people have no problem with paedophiles, rapists and the like going to hell. That's not a problem.

That would be justice.

But God doesn't differentiate between sinners. Sin is lawlessness and we all fall into that category. That's a bitter pill to swallow. Here's an even more bitter one. *Some paedophiles and rapists will be in heaven.* They will get to enjoy the glories of living with God for eternity. And some of their victims will be worshipping Jesus side by side with them. Even more incredibly, they will be thanking Jesus that they are there with them.

I mean, that is just scandalous! There is a verse in a famous hymn that says, *'The vilest offender who truly believes, that moment from Jesus a pardon receives.'* For many years I refused to sing that verse. I refused to believe that God would do that to me. That there was still an opportunity for my abuser to go to heaven.

There was no way that I would accept any of this ever.

Ever.

Until I had a *complete change of heart.*

What I've learned as a pastor is that God saves anybody and everybody *He chooses.* He doesn't ask for my opinion. He doesn't ask for your opinion. We don't get to decide who is worthy and who is not.

Do I think that child abusers, *who accept the gospel of Jesus*, will be in heaven?

Yes.

Do I think that some victims of abuse, who've worked hard all their lives to get over it, have never been in trouble with the law, and give to charity, *but reject the gospel of Jesus*, will be in hell?

Yes.

HOW CAN I BELIEVE THESE THINGS AFTER EVERYTHING THAT HAPPENED TO ME?

W ell, it was a process. It took a lot of time and a lot of painful self-reflection to change both my *heart* and my *mind*. It certainly didn't happen overnight.

Here's how I got there.

Firstly, I came to *accept the truth* of the good news about Jesus Christ.

I believe that Jesus Christ really existed. He walked the earth a little over two thousand years ago.

> I believe that He was fully God and fully man. In fact, He was the perfect, sinless God-Man.
> I believe that He was born of a virgin and lived a life of complete obedience to the will of the Father.
> I believe that He was illegally tried and sentenced to death.
> I believe He went to His death willingly.
> I believe that on that cross He took upon Himself the full wrath of God against sin.

I believe that He literally died.

I believe that three days later He literally rose again from the grave.

I believe that He appeared to many hundreds of witnesses before ascending to heaven where He now sits at the right hand of God the Father.

I believe that He is coming back for His people one day.

I believe that when He does return, God's perfect and final justice will be executed on all humanity.

I believe that faith in Him is the *only way* we can have peace with God in this life.

Secondly, I came to believe some *bad news* about myself.

All have sinned and fall short of the glory of God. **(Romans 3:23)**

My abusers and tormentors were definitely sinners. But, *so was I.*

Despite my terrible childhood, I was still responsible to God for my personal sin and rebellion against God and His holiness.

I came to realise that I'd spent far too many years blaming my stepmother, her friends and a whole host of others for the mess that was my life. I had expended all of my energy on people who didn't care one iota about me or my life. They had all moved on with theirs while I was stuck in a nightmarish time-loop replaying the abuse in my head over and over again.

I could see their sins easily enough. I could point their faults out in the minutest of detail. I was their judge, jury and executioner. But what good had it done me? My soul was rotten to the core. My whole life reeked of bitterness and paranoia.

I pretended everything was OK, but inside I was miserable and depressed. I felt so alone that I physically ached from it.

And, ironically, I came to see how blind I had been.

Not only had I been blind to the truth about Jesus, but I had been blind to my own sins and faults. Oh, I knew they were there. But I had ready-made excuses for my defects. *I was a victim! I had been through trauma!* That was my get-out-of-jail-free card for every occasion that my conscience troubled me. If that didn't work, then I could always be placated by my social workers and counsellors who were only too happy to spoon-feed me the same philosophy.

They told me I wasn't a bad person, even though I knew I was.

They told me that my bad decisions were the results of a chaotic childhood when, in fact, they were also often the result of my own foolishness.

They told me that the answers to my *issues* lay within me, when I clearly knew that wasn't true.

They told me I needed to love myself more, when in reality I needed to love myself less.

They tickled my ears and said all the things I wanted to hear.

Yet I knew deep down that it was all untrue.

Thirdly, I ran headlong into the Bible.

A book I'd scorned, though never read. A book I had long believed was stupid and irrelevant. In fact, the more I read it the more it beat me up and down the street with truth bomb after truth bomb.

I was a mess and it hurt to have to really look inside myself.

It stung me to the core of my being as it forensically picked apart my excuses for denying God. His Word ransacked my soul, discarding all the rubbish, waste and bile that I had been storing up for decades. It made me take stock of my life. It forced me to look in a spiritual mirror and see what I had become.

Regardless of my many excuses, it confronted me with my sinful, selfish nature. I, like everybody around me, lived under the mistaken assumption that God graded people on how good they were in this life. Obviously, as a victim I was near the top of His list. In my mind, I got a free pass to a heaven I didn't even believe in! Rapists and child abusers were at the bottom of the list. They went straight to a hell I didn't even believe in!

No questions asked. No doubts at all.

But, more importantly, the Bible taught me that *all* have sinned and fall short of the glory of God. It didn't matter if you were doing life for murder or taught a Sunday School class. God, through His Word, taught me that *sin at its basest level is lawlessness*. It taught me that hard though my childhood had been, traumatic though my experiences in life had been, *I was still a rebel against a holy God.*

I was devastated by this.

No, it didn't feel fair. But that didn't make it untrue.

Yes, they were horrible truths to face. But that didn't make them untrue.

I stopped judging my abusers and started judging *myself*.

I stopped grading my *'goodness'* against my abusers and, instead, judged myself against Jesus.

And I came up so, so short, it was ridiculous.

Of course, this process took time. It clearly didn't happen in the time that it took me to write this book, or for you to read this chapter. But, once I had cleared away all the deadwood of my excuses, I was left with one absolute certainty.

I was a sinner in need of God's salvation.

So here I was, convinced that Jesus died for sinners, taking upon himself the full wrath of God.

Here I was, convinced that I, by Jesus' standards, was a sinner heading toward a lost eternity in hell.

What was I supposed to do now?

REPENT

noun: *repentance;* **plural noun:** *repentances*

> *the action of repenting; sincere regret or remorse. 'Each person who turns to God in genuine repentance and faith will be saved.'*

synonyms:

> Remorse, contrition, contriteness, penitence, sorrow, sorrowfulness, regret, ruefulness, remorsefulness, pangs of conscience, prickings of conscience, shame, guilt, self-reproach, self-condemnation, compunction.

I have not come to call the righteous but sinners to repentance.

(Jesus)

Repentance is a discovery of the evil of sin, a mourning that we have committed it, a resolution to forsake it. It is, in fact, a change of mind of a very deep and practical character, which makes the man love what once he hated, and hate what once he loved.

(Charles Spurgeon)

As I battled through the demons of my childhood, I was acutely aware that I had no power no change myself, no matter how hard I tried. I, like millions of others, lied to myself on a daily basis. We tell ourselves that we are going to get better. We are going to do better. This year will be our year. We tell ourselves that this relationship is going to be different. This one will fulfil us. We tell ourselves a thousand little lies but the cold, hard truth is that we just can't get the horror out of our minds.

We are crippled by it.

The people who damaged us are not going to change either. Even if they go to jail. Even if we see justice. We could beat them, humiliate them, even kill them and it wouldn't change what has happened, or is happening to us, one little bit.

I had been waiting all my life for other people to repent of what they had done to me, when, all along, it was God who required repentance from me.

Many people are confused about what repentance means. Some think it's to feel sorry or remorseful whereas, biblically, the word means *'to change your mind'*. Repentance is key to understanding the good news about Jesus, and how we should respond to it.

When the gospel was preached in the early church, Peter told the crowd in **Acts 3:19,** *'Repent, then, and turn to God, so that your sins may be wiped out, that times of refreshing may come from the Lord.'* In other words, change your mind about Jesus and your sin. Stop blaming other people for your mistakes. Stop blaming them for your behaviour. Stop blaming your childhood for your hard-heartedness.

Now, I don't say this stuff lightly. When I first heard these words, I was angry. *'Repent!' I thought. 'Repent! What do I have to say sorry for? People should be repenting to me!'* But I had to get past that. Jesus would deal with that in time, but God required repentance from me as I accepted the good news about Jesus. Without repentance there would be no salvation.

This was a real kick in the gut to me as I wrestled through these things. I had hidden behind my victimhood for so long that I had grown comfortable with it. It was so much a part of me that letting it go and taking responsibility for my own life was a real wrench. I wanted God to sort out my issues before offering Him allegiance, whereas God demanded my repentance first and foremost. My personal issues, important as they were, came a very distant second to God's requirements.

I had to come to a place where I realised that my whole view of the world was warped and wrong. My whole view of God needed to change completely. I needed to stop seeing Him as the enemy and see myself as a rebel before Him. I no longer wanted to live my life on my terms, I wanted to live it on God's. I wanted to follow Jesus instead of my own selfish desires. I wanted some peace in my heart and my mind and I realised I wasn't getting that by living as if God didn't exist.

Even this act of contrition was a gift from God.

As I prayed to Jesus for help, God mercifully granted me repentance in Him.

All of this led to a change of thinking, a change of lifestyle, and a change of heart. True repentance always produces what the Bible calls spiritual fruit. In other words, the genuineness of my repentance would be seen in the way I would live my life from that moment on. I could not be the centre of my world anymore. My feelings could not guide my life and my decisions anymore.

I changed my mind about God and Jesus, accepted my sin, and handed everything over to His care.

God was giving me a clean slate.

Praise be to the God and Father of our Lord Jesus Christ! In his great mercy he has given us new birth into a living hope through the resurrection of Jesus Christ from the dead. **(1 Peter 1:3)**

A CLEAN SLATE

How often do we sit in darkness at night and wish that we could change our lives? To swap our memories for somebody else's?

For a clean slate? A fresh start? A do-over?

Well, the good news is that we can! We can start afresh with God. We can have a new heart. A new way of thinking. A new family.

A *new* and *living* hope.

It starts with accepting *who we are* before God. It comes through acceptance of the fact that, inside, we are not a pretty sight. We may well have perfected the art of smiling and pretending all is OK with the world. But, when the last person goes home, and we are all alone with our thoughts, *we know* that we are sinners.

Again, I know, that your instant reaction to that sentence is probably to jump to your own defence. But, can I counsel you to fight the urge that wants you to pass the buck? We have to fight that inclination inside us that says, *'Yes, but...'* Or, *'What about...?'*

Our *only* option when we see ourselves as the Bible sees us is to bow the knee to King Jesus. That gigantic step will lead us into a whole new world. It will lead us into a whole new way of thinking.

It will give us a whole new heart.

I know. I know. It sounds scarcely believable. It sounds too good to be true. Or maybe it sounds ridiculous to you. In **Hebrews 13:5 (ESV)** God makes this promise to all those who repent of their sin and turn to Jesus for salvation:

> I will never leave you nor forsake you.

> Reach out to Jesus.
> He will not cast you away.
> He will not humiliate you.
> He will not hurt you.
> He will not let you down.
> He offers you a clean slate.

Jesus came for the victims. For the helpless. For the abused. For the lost. For the wayward. For those without a voice. For those who've faced injustice. For those who've known only pain and hurt.

For the abuser. For the oppressor. For the violent. For the murderers. For the rapists. For the paedophiles. For those who have only caused pain and hurt.

> For broken people like *me*.
> For broken people like *you*.
> For broken people like **them**.

I had to come to a place in my life where I realised that I was a sinner before a Holy God. Yes, I had been a victim – there's no doubt about that. Yes, serious crimes had been committed against me. No, I was not to blame for any of it.

But God was asking me a different set of questions.

Was I responsible for my own rebellion against Him? Yes. Even though I desperately wanted to blame her. I wanted to hang it all on her. *'I would have followed you, God, if **she** hadn't...'* Learning that I was *solely responsible* for my own sinful rebellion against God was a tough one. I'm not going to lie. It hurt. A lot.

But I had chosen to stick two fingers up at God. I had chosen to lie, cheat, steal, hurt and manipulate people. I told myself that I wasn't like her.

Yet, in so many ways I was *exactly* like **her**.

I was hard-hearted, bitter, cruel and angry. I was every inch the sinner that the Bible called me out to be. It took me more self-harm, more drug-fuelled parties, more violence, more crime and a cell in a maximum-security prison to finally help me to see the truth:

I was a sinner before a just and holy God and *I had no excuses*.

The hard truth is that I wasn't entirely a victim. In fact, I had often been the victimiser that I so hated about her. I was a rebel and, what's more, I was proud of it. But where had it gotten me? All this rage. All this bitterness. All this self-destruction.

It had gotten me nowhere.

It had led me to throwing away the best part of a decade of my life – trying to hurt her, blaming the world, and yet only succeeding in damaging myself more and more.

I soon realised that I needed the Lord in my life. I needed some outside help. Social workers hadn't helped me. Counsellors hadn't helped me. Youth workers hadn't helped me. Family members couldn't help me. They were all busy fighting their own demons. I needed some outside supernatural help to turn my life around.

So, in desperation, I threw my lot in with Jesus.

I sat on a park bench, admitted my sinful rebellion against God and threw myself on the mercy of Jesus. Nothing fancy. Nothing profound was said. Just a quiet prayer from a desperate man, limping through life with an ache in his soul that he couldn't fill no matter how hard he tried. I laid aside all pretence that I was 'OK' when the reality was that I was anything but. I laid aside my tough exterior. I lowered the ramparts to my soul, and Jesus walked across the stone bridge of my heart and took up residence.

I was broken, terrified, anxious but hopeful that He could help me rebuild my car crash of a life.

Instead of Jesus being irrelevant to my life, He now became the focus of it. Instead of thinking about myself and my own pain, I began to think of Him and His.

> *Yes, I was abused.* **Jesus was abused more**.
> *Yes, I was humiliated.* **Jesus was humiliated more**.
> *Yes, I was rejected.* **Jesus was rejected more**.

I came to realise that my suffering and pain, real though it was, paled into insignificance in the face of Jesus and His great sacrifice.

It didn't stop my pain. It didn't lessen the impact of my struggles. But it did offer me a context in which I could handle my emotions without them drowning me completely.

Then, one day, completely out of the blue, I noticed that something had changed.

Something deep inside me.

I began to care for people; to love them.

Even people I would previously have hated.

LOVE

YORKSHIRE, 1982

There it was again, that creaking on the stairs. I knew what was coming next. It was the same message almost every night.

'You know that nobody loves you, right? That's why your real mother dumped you on me. That's why your dad is hardly ever home. Nobody loves you and nobody ever will.'

Love was a difficult concept for me to understand. After all, growing up, I don't remember a single person in my life telling me that they loved me. I was never affirmed. I was often criticised. I was always demeaned. I was never hugged by my parents or those in charge of my care.

The only physical contact with adults, more often than not, would result in pain for me.

That meant I was wary of everybody as I entered adulthood. For many years afterward, I automatically flinched when anybody raised their arms or made sudden movements near me. I had friends, but not at any deep level. I'd loved a couple of girls but, like everything else in my miserable life, it ended in heartbreak.

I just didn't know *how* to love. I didn't know *how* to process my emotions. I knew fear, hope, despair and anger. I had those down pat. Love, on the other hand, was a great mystery to me.

I suppose that was the reason that I didn't really know how to respond when Christians asked me if I loved Jesus. The truth was that I had no idea if I loved Him. I accepted that He loved me, although if I'm honest I didn't really understand what it meant. It said it in the Bible, so I figured that it must be true.

But, in reality, I didn't *feel* anything for Jesus.

There was no emotional attachment on my part. Not anything I could describe as love anyway. But, then again, what was love? It began to trouble me. To gnaw away at me. What *did* love **feel** like? What was it *supposed* to feel like? I asked lots of Christians, but they just appeared bemused by my questions.

People would often quote **1 John 3:16** at me. *'This is how we know what love is: Jesus Christ laid down his life for us.'* Christians would talk of the great joy and peace they felt in accepting God's love. Again, honestly, I didn't have a clue what they were talking about. When I had repented of my sin and dedicated my life to following Jesus, there was no big emotional release. There was no deep sense of joy in my spirit. I didn't feel bathed in the love of the Almighty. I didn't feel much of anything.

I just felt numb.

But, I did want to *please* God. I did want to *obey* the teachings of Jesus. More than anything else, I was prepared to do *anything* and *everything* necessary in my life to show God how serious I was about my new-found faith. I stopped taking drugs. I stopped maliciously hurting people. I stopped feeling sorry for myself. I began to focus more and more on Jesus. I began to study the Bible seriously.

And a miraculous thing happened.

Not overnight. But, as the months and years wore on. The more I considered Jesus, the less I considered myself. The more I considered His pain, the more my own pain was put into perspective. Slowly but surely, my emotions began changing. In fact, my feelings caught up to the truth I was believing.

I discovered that the secret to my emotional and spiritual healing didn't lie with other people. Nor did it lie within me. The secret to a joyful life had nothing to do with my enemies getting their just desserts.

Becoming calm and less angry inside came out of a growing relationship with Jesus. My heart was softening, and my soul was being cleansed of all the dirt and bitterness that had held it captive for so many years. Instead of allowing my demons to camp inside my head and heart, Jesus moved in full-time.

Instead of being shaped and formed by my own pain, I began to be shaped and formed by understanding His. I came to understand that true peace and healing can only come about when a soul has been captured by Jesus.

And when a life has been fully submitted to His will.

I discovered that the answers to all my *whys* were tied up in the answers to all His whys. *Why did He come to earth? Why did He allow Himself to be humiliated? Why put Himself through the torture of being rejected by His own creation? Why allow the Jewish leaders to unjustly arrest Him? Why allow Himself to be scorned by His friends and His neighbours? Why risk the rejection of His earthly family? Why take upon Himself the full wrath of God the Father?*

> A **love** so grand, so immense, I still struggle to comprehend it.

I'll probably still be struggling to explain it a thousand years from now. The Father loving us so much He sent His only Son. The Son loving His Father so much He comes to earth and puts Himself through the absolute horror and trauma of the cross.

I discovered that there is a far greater love to be found in a relationship with Jesus than there is pain and anguish to be found inside me.

> *What kind of love is this*
> *That gave itself for me*
> *I am the guilty one*
> *Yet I go free;*
> *What kind of love is this*
> *A love I've never known*
> *I didn't even know his name*
> *What kind of love is this?*[1]

All this is great, but it still left me with the problem of my childhood abusers and tormentors. How could I ever bring myself to accept that they could be welcomed into the church and even into heaven itself?

One word...

1   'What Kind of Love is This', Bryn and Sally Haworth, © 2002 Bella Music Ltd.

GRACE

For by grace you have been saved through faith, and that not of yourselves; it is the gift of God.
(Ephesians 2:8 NKJV)

No one was ever saved because his sins were small; no one was ever rejected on account of the greatness of his sins. Where sin abounded, grace shall much more abound.
(Archibald Alexander)

I understood the concept of justice when I became a Christian. **Justice was getting what you deserved**. So, for instance, when I was sentenced to prison for slashing two men, that was justice being served. I deserved to go to prison. I had committed the crime.

God's justice would be served by all sinners going to hell.

I also understood mercy. I understood that **mercy was getting something you didn't deserve**. I remember when I was sentenced for burglary as a teenager and justice demanded a custodial sentence. However, a judge showed mercy on me and sentenced me to community service.

God's mercy offers us full forgiveness despite the fact we deserve to go to hell.

Grace, on the other hand, took some getting used to. Because grace means not only am I saved from hell, but He will continue to bless me for all eternity. When He saved me, God gave me a new spirit. He gave me a new heart. He gave me a wonderful wife. He gave me my beautiful girls. He gave me an amazing church family, made up of friends from all around the globe. He gave me back my dignity and self-respect. He saved me from myself. He has given me abundant life.

God's grace is when He gives us what we don't deserve.

In the early years I had no real understanding of how far God's grace extended. I knew I didn't deserve to go to heaven. I always felt out of place in the church. The people dressed nicely and spoke politely. They all seemed so respectable. I used to wonder what I was doing there. I was an ex-con with a bad drug habit and a huge chip on my shoulder. I couldn't understand why God would save me and why the church would embrace me.

As I grew to love the Lord more and more and the church more and more I became scared. What if people found out what I was really like? What a liar I was. What a fantasist. What if they realised that I had done some truly awful things in my life? I thought about a lot of my victims over the years. The people I had stabbed. The homes I had burgled. The drugs I had sold. The frauds I had committed.

I dreaded people who knew me in the past coming into the church to expose me as a charlatan. I used to have nightmares of all the people I had ever hurt coming to a church service and sitting there listening as I told them of my new life in Jesus.

I could see their sneers. I could hear their jeering. I could sense the anger, hostility and cynicism. What a joke! A lying rat like me hanging around respectable people and pretending to be a Christian. It sounded ridiculous to me, and I knew I was genuine!

Then one day I discovered these verses in the Bible in **Romans 5:6-8 NKJV**:

> *For when we were still without strength, in due time Christ died for the ungodly. For scarcely for a righteous man will one die; yet perhaps for a good man someone would even dare to die. But God demonstrates His own love toward us, in that while we were still sinners, Christ died for us.*

I discovered that Jesus didn't just die for me. But He did it *knowing just how ungodly I was*. He saved me when I was at my weakest. When I was at my least desirable. He saw me at my worst and still saved me. He didn't reach out to me because He saw some redeemable feature in me, like my fantastic sense of humour! There was nothing lovable about me. There was no good in me. Instead, His own love compelled him to do it.

The sense of freedom and relief that passage brought me was profound. No, the people in the church didn't know what I was truly like, but Jesus did. Yes, people I had hurt could sneer and question my motives, but Jesus had still died for me. They couldn't change that. I couldn't change that. Satan himself couldn't change it.

> *Amazing Grace, how sweet the sound*
> *That saved a wretch like me*
> *I once was lost, but now am found*
> *was blind but now I see.*
> **(John Newton)**

Jesus was in the business of saving wretches and He saved this wretch right here. I had no idea why. It was mind-blowing. I learned of the extent of His grace by contemplating **Ephesians 2:4-9 NKJV**:

> God, who is rich in mercy, because of His great love with which He loved us, even when we were dead in trespasses, **made us alive** together with Christ (by grace you have been saved), and raised us up together, and **made us sit together** in the heavenly places in Christ Jesus, that in the ages to come He might show the exceeding riches of His grace in His kindness toward us in Christ Jesus. For by grace you have been saved through faith, and that **not of yourselves; it is the gift of God**, **not of works, lest anyone should boast**.

I was so blind. I was so lost. I was so dead in my sins. It was only when God made me alive in Jesus and granted me the gift of salvation that I truly began to change.

I slowly began to realise that if God was that merciful and gracious toward me, then He could be gracious and merciful to whomever He pleased.

He could even show grace to **her**.

But there was an even more bitter pill to swallow.

THE BITTERSWEET PILL OF GOD'S SOVEREIGNTY

No doctrine in the whole of mankind has more excited
the hatred of mankind than the truth of the absolute
sovereignty of God.
(Charles Spurgeon)

Christians like to throw around little phrases and complicated words. The most popular of them is 'Sovereignty'. They forever talk about the 'Sovereignty of God'. In effect, they are trying to communicate that God is in control of all things.

In other words, life is not random chance. Things do not happen to us accidentally. The evil that happens is under His control. God even works in and through evil people.

He Himself is not evil, nor is He the author of evil.

But He does use evil people for the purposes of good. Now, some people don't like this. I didn't like it when I first heard it. But, like most things difficult to hear, I came to understand and appreciate it as my knowledge of God and the Bible deepened. In **Isaiah 45:7** God says this about Himself: '*I form the light and create darkness, **I bring prosperity and create disaster**; I, the LORD, do all these things.*'

Isaiah is not teaching us that God sins.

God cannot sin.

He is saying that even evil is not outside of God's control. God uses all the evil in the world for the purposes of *His good*. In other words, there is nothing happening to us in our lives, no matter how evil it may be, that is outside of the control of Almighty God.

Hang on a moment.

> *Am I saying that God permits child abuse and all sorts of other perverted evil?*

Yes. He does.

> *How can this be true? How can I believe in a God like this?*

Well, let's think about the most evil act in the history of the world.

> *The crucifixion.*

Sinless Jesus murdered by evil sinners. Yet, listen to what God says about it in **Isaiah 53:10**:

> Yet ***it was the Lord's will to crush him and cause him to suffer***, *and though the Lord makes his life an offering for sin, he will see his offspring and prolong his days, and the will of the Lord will prosper in his hand.*

The deliberate **will** of God crushed Jesus and caused Him to suffer. We are offended by this. We are scandalised by it, despite the fact that the early church fathers accepted it unhesitatingly. When the Apostle Peter, for example, was preaching his first sermon after Jesus had ascended into heaven, he said this to the crowd in **Acts 2:23**: '*This man was handed over to you* **by God's deliberate plan and foreknowledge;** *and you, with the help of wicked men, put him to death by nailing him to the cross.*'

Listen to the prayer of Peter and John just after they were released from prison in **Acts 4:27-28**. *'Indeed Herod and Pontius Pilate met together with the Gentiles and the people of Israel in this city to conspire against your holy servant Jesus, whom you anointed.* **They did what your power and will had decided beforehand should happen.'**

The crucifixion of Jesus looked like the biggest miscarriage of justice in history. It looked like God was asleep at the wheel. It looked like He didn't care. When in fact, *His was the hidden hand behind it all.* Now, I appreciate that many people don't like this. They can't bring themselves to accept that God permits evil to happen. But God is sovereign over all things.

> Even over our abuse.
> *Especially* over our abuse.

Lamentations 3:37–39 puts it more starkly: *'Who can speak and have it happen if the Lord has not decreed it?* **Is it not from the mouth of the Most High that both calamities and good things come?** *Why should any living man complain when punished for his sins?'*

It sounds terrible, doesn't it? If you are hearing this for the first time, then I can imagine your shock and horror. I can imagine you instinctively recoiling at what I am writing. I couldn't believe it myself, at first. But, is God only sovereign over the good things that happen to us in this life? Not according to **Ecclesiastes 7:14**: *'When times are good, be happy; but when times are bad, consider this: God has made the one as well as the other.'*

As I considered it more and more, as I studied the Bible more and more, my distaste decreased and my comfort increased. Instead of being mortified by this doctrine, it brought me peace.

I wept to think that my suffering had not been in vain. That senseless though it had been to me, it was not senseless in the light of eternity. God is not impersonal. He hasn't just set the world in motion and left us to our own devices.

He is intimately involved in the world.

God may have ordained evil in our world, but He does not revel in it. He does not approve of it or take satisfaction in it. In fact, He can use any situation in the world, no matter how terrible, and ultimately bring good out of it.

Really? God uses child abuse to bring glory for His own name?

That's the Christian answer?

Tell that to three-year-old John, gang-raped by all the male members of his family over a ten-year period.

Tell that to five-year-old Jane, forced to have sex with all of her mother's lovers.

Tell that to four-year-old Paula, forced to go to a slaughterhouse and warned that the same would happen to her and her three siblings if she told on the man who was molesting them all.

Tell that to Phil, a faithful pastor who discovered that one of his church members had raped his six-year-old son multiple times.

Tell that to two-year-old Sally, forced to sing Christmas carols as a child while her dad and uncles took it in turns to rape her over almost 15 years.

Tell that to seven-year-old Raphael whose mother sold him to pimps in northern Brazil so she could feed the rest of the family.

Tell it to my terrified twelve-year-old self, after suffering a decade of starvation, beatings and abuse.

That's what we will tell them?

'God allowed that to happen to you. But, don't worry, he has a plan.'

Really?

What they, and we, need to know is that what happened to them was **WRONG**. It was **EVIL** and *God hates it*.

As they get older we need to, very carefully and very gently, show them that this is the result of the fall of the human race in the garden of Eden. Evil and perversion everywhere. Yet, God still works for good in the world, despite the terrors of it. Yes, the world is perverse, but it is not as bad as it could be – and it doesn't come close to God's coming wrath. They need to know that there will be a day of judgement for all of their abusers. They will get what's coming to them.

But, that day of judgement will be for all humanity – *us included*.

We need to tell them the story of Joseph, which we find in the book of **Genesis**, the first book of the Bible. The story of a young boy whose brothers, out of sheer, evil jealousy, beat him up, throw him down a well and then sell him into slavery. Poor Joseph gets into all sorts of bother, before finally ending up doing over a decade in jail. The lad has done nothing wrong up until this point. Well, he was a bit of a show-off, but he'd done nothing deserving this kind of treatment. The only reason he was even in jail was for trying to obey God's Word. Look where that got him!

Anyway, his story takes a turn for the better and, by a remarkable turn of events, he ends up becoming the governor of Egypt, second only in authority to Pharaoh. He goes from a bloody mess in a well, slavery and jail, to being one of the most powerful men in one of the most powerful empires in the world at that time.

Talk about a turnaround.

Joseph never forgot his family and how they had treated him. But, over the years, as God worked in his heart, he began to soften toward them. And one day, as providence would have it, they all met again. The brothers were obviously terrified when they realised just who Joseph was and how powerful he had become. He could have had them all sentenced to death in a heartbeat after what they'd put him through (I know I would have). Instead, this is what he said to his brothers in **Genesis 50:20**: *'You intended to harm me, but God intended it for good to accomplish what is now being done, the saving of many lives.'*

Joseph's experiences hadn't made him bitter toward God. In fact, they'd done the opposite. The knowledge that God was absolutely sovereign over his life, *including his suffering*, gave him comfort and allowed him to show mercy to those who deserved none.

God had allowed that situation to happen. He wasn't the cause of it, but He had permitted it. While the devil was intending to destroy Joseph through the evil desires of his brothers, God used the horrors of what had happened to Joseph to bless not only his own family, but a whole nation. Of course, this didn't ease Joseph's trauma. He still suffered. It probably didn't stop his feelings of rejection and pain. It probably stung him to the core that his own family would do that to him. But a strong belief in God's absolute sovereignty over every detail of his life, *good and bad*, at least gave meaning and purpose to his experiences.

In other words, Joseph's suffering wasn't meaningless. His trauma wasn't just random bad luck. What happened to him *did* matter. It wasn't without a purpose. So much *good* came out of it for so many people.

I know it may sound ridiculous to you right now. It might even sound offensive. But, like Joseph, like myself, like so many other abuse sufferers in the church, we can testify to you that *good can come out of your sufferings and traumas.*

If I could gather all of my abusers, mental, physical, sexual and emotional, into a room so I could talk to them all at once, I would say this. *'What you meant for evil, God planned for good.'* Now, don't get me wrong. I would be shaking. I would be nauseous. Actually, I would feel sick to the pit of my stomach.

But it would be completely true.

They wouldn't have to understand it or even accept it. That's not the point. In Christ, I can now step back and see the bigger picture. And the bigger picture is that God has my best interests at heart.

Without them and their evil influence in my life, this book would not be in your hands. Without the pain and trauma I went through in my late teens and early 20's, unsuccessfully trying to process my childhood, I doubt I would have ever entered a church.

In fact, *my pain was one of the chief means God used to draw me to Jesus.*

Yes, that thought still blows my mind every single day.

Nor would I be the man I am today without those people. I wouldn't be the father I am, or the husband I am. I wouldn't be the pastor I am. I'd still be lost. I'd still be angry about my childhood. I'd still be depressed. I'd still be anxious. I'd still be paranoid. I'd still have a massive chip on my shoulder (for those who think I still do, trust me, it has shrunk an awful lot!). But, most likely, like many of my childhood friends, I'd still be in prison, on the streets or dead.

Many years ago, my dad said to me: *'I am proud of you, son. Turning your life around like this.'* I remember it clearly. Keziah, my eldest, had just been born and he was visiting me at the church I was ministering in at the time. I remember saying to him:

'Dad. Don't be proud of me. I'll tell you where my efforts got me. They got me a drug habit. They left me on the streets. They left me angry and depressed; then, finally, they got me a jail cell. Everything good in my life now, Dad, is down to God. Every single thing. I promise you 100%. Jesus saved me, Dad. He saved me, and He's the one who has turned my life around.'

He just grunted at me and I could see the confusion writ large on his face. He didn't have a clue what I was saying. He didn't understand a single thing. It just sounded like spiritual gobbledygook to him. Regardless, he had to admit that something had happened to me. Something had caused my life to turn around dramatically. Something had stopped me from continuing down my path toward self-destruction. Something has kept me off drugs and married for over 20 years.

He thought it was my own effort and industry. That I'd somehow magically pulled myself together.

But he was dead wrong.

It was 100% God Almighty and the work of Jesus in my life.

If God did that for me, then believe me, He can do it for you, too.

GOD'S WAYS ARE NOT OUR WAYS

'For my thoughts are not your thoughts, neither are your ways my ways,' declares the Lord. 'As the heavens are higher than the earth, so are my ways higher than your ways and my thoughts than your thoughts.'
(Isaiah 55:8-9)

The more I understand about how God works in the world, the more I understand that He uses *whomever He likes, how He likes, whenever He likes*. If God wants to use unbelievers to fulfil His plans for the world, then *He will, and He does*. Some of the people God has used greatly throughout history have been total idiots. Noah used to get off his nut on wine. Moses was a killer with no faith, and a bad stutter. Rahab was a prostitute. King David, another killer and adulterer. Jonah was a bottle merchant. Matthew was a scumbag loan shark . The Apostle Paul was a stone-cold killer.

We wouldn't have voted for any of them in an election. We wouldn't have invited any of them to be the pastor of our church or to be a part of our church internship programme. Yet, God took losers like this, and used them to accomplish His purposes.

In effect, I soon came to realise that God has His finger on the pulse of *everything* in this world, no matter how small and unimportant it seemed to me. Recently, for example, Scotland voted against independence. Did I like that? No. I voted in favour of it. But when the result came in I accepted it as God's will.

He doesn't make mistakes.

We worship a God who *made* all things, *knows* all things and *created* all things. He does not work according to our feeble little minds. He is far above us and far beyond what even the greatest mind can comprehend. Often, when *we* look at the world around us we see a mess. God, on the other hand, does not have the same perspective as us. From his lofty, eternal perch, *all things* are working toward *His* ultimate purpose. We may not see it now, we may not understand it now, and we don't even have to agree with it, but God is working in such a way that one day people will realise that He is the Lord and there is no other.

Remember this: God works in surprising ways.

> *The incarnation.* **A shock.**
> *The virgin birth.* **A shock.**
> *The God-Man dying a humiliating death on a cross.* **A shock.**
> *Jesus rising from the dead.* **A shock**.

If we'd been given the job of redeeming the world, how many of these things would we have planned?

Exactly.

We just don't understand so much of what God does. He is not taken aback by anything that is going on in our world right now. There's not a person or a power that will thwart Him.

THE BAD, THE UGLY, AND THE BROKEN

God chose the foolish things of the world to shame the wise; God chose the weak things of the world to shame the strong.

(1 Corinthians 1:27)

You may be broken by your past right now. You might feel useless, because that's how you were always made to feel. You might look in the mirror and think you're good for nothing. You might be good for nothing. You might have had terrible things done to you. You may have done terrible things to other people. But God uses the useless, the fearful, the broken, the despised, the weak and the foolish.

Yes, He even uses evil people. Because that's what we all were until He rescued us.

But the Christian life doesn't stop there. There is more…

FORGIVENESS

Forgiveness is like this: a room can be dank because you have closed the windows, you've closed the curtains. But the sun is shining outside, and the air is fresh outside. In order to get that fresh air, you have to get up and open the window and draw the curtains apart.

(Desmond Tutu)

When I first read **Romans 12:19** I was very disappointed. *'Do not take revenge, my dear friends, but leave room for God's wrath, for it is written: "It is mine to avenge; I will repay," says the Lord.'* I wanted to have salvation *and* hold on to my hatred. I soon discovered that the two were not compatible with the Christian life.

I had carried the twin brothers of bitterness and resentment with me for so long, it was almost as if they were a part of me. Who would I be without them? What would I be like? Where would all my raw emotion go? *'OK,'* I told myself. *'I will leave it to the Lord to repay. But I will never forgive them. I don't care what anybody says. It will never happen.'*

Foolishness.

Thankfully, for me God's Holy Spirit was far stronger than my feeble will. His patience consumed my impatience. His love and forbearance relentlessly chipped away at my anger and bitterness. **Galatians 5:22-23** tells us, *'The fruit of the Spirit is love, joy, peace, forbearance, kindness, goodness, faithfulness, gentleness and self-control.'* God's Word was clear: There could be no room in my life for the Holy Spirit and my old way of thinking and behaving. If the fruit of the Spirit's work in my life was these things, then the fruit of my old life was made even clearer in **Galatians 5:19-21.** *'The acts of the flesh are obvious: sexual immorality, impurity and debauchery; idolatry and witchcraft; hatred, discord, jealousy, fits of rage, selfish ambition, dissensions, factions and envy; drunkenness, orgies, and the like.'*

I realised that I could not change. I needed His help to change me. I realised that by not forgiving my abusers I was in fact hurting myself and grieving the Holy Spirit of God. Martin Luther put it like this: *'You can't keep the birds from flying over your head but you can keep them from building a nest in your hair.'*

Every time I thought of her and my tormentors, even years after **she** was no longer a part of my life, it was like **she** still had control of me. The feelings of terror welled up, quickly followed by the red mist of anger. I don't have the words, three decades later, to adequately explain how sick **she**, in particular, made me feel.

I tried to forgive her. I tried to pray for her, but the roots of bitterness ran deep. My hurts were so, so many. I tried to be Christian about it but my heart wasn't in it. I told myself that God would let me off. After all, He knows what **she** did to me. He knows what the others did too. How much I was hurt and humiliated. *'Surely, I am allowed to hate her. I'll forgive the others as long as I can hate her.'* That's what I told myself. And then, the passage of time wore on and memories faded, as they so often do. The scars were still there. A certain smell or someone's tone transported me back to childhood nightmares. But, over time, I became more and more adept at putting it out of my mind.

I had my own children now. And I would protect them to the death. No one would hurt them. They would never know my kind of pain. They would grow up in a home that was loving, stable and secure.

Jesus would rule our home.

As a pastor I would be confronted with passages in the Bible like **Ephesians 4:32**: *'Be kind and compassionate to one another, forgiving each other, just as in Christ God forgave you.'* Of course, **she** would pop into my mind, but I pushed the thoughts down. I told myself that if we ever met then I would put this into practice, knowing full well that the chances of that were very slim indeed. I did Bible studies on verses like **Luke 6:28,** *'Bless those who curse you, pray for those who mistreat you.'* Maybe, once or twice in two decades, I did pray for her, but even then, it was grudgingly, asked without faith or conviction. Just so that I could feel better about myself. Then there was **Matthew 5:43-44,** *'You have heard that it was said, "Love your neighbour and hate your enemy." But I tell you, love your enemies and pray for those who persecute you.'* That was just for Christians being persecuted, I told myself. It wasn't for her and my other childhood tormentors. But it was for *her*, and what is more, I knew it.

I *knew* it.

In **Colossians 3:13** God commands the church, *'Bear with each other and forgive one another if any of you has a grievance against* *someone. **Forgive as the Lord forgave you.'*** What an absolute sickener that verse was, and still is, for me. I knew from that very moment that I had a duty to God to forgive these people.

I'd like to finish the book by telling you that I sought *her* out, and the others, and in a glorious Hollywood ending, we met, embraced warmly, and that **she** is now a member of my church.

But we never met.

I found out online that **she**, along with another of my abusers, had died. The night I discovered this I couldn't sleep, and the end result was the blog post you read at the outset of this book.

I was so conflicted. I was relieved that **she** was dead. I was hopeful that **she** would be in hell. I felt guilty because I knew that I should be more merciful toward her. I felt sad that **she** died without speaking to me. I wondered if **she** had thought about me and my sister in her final days and hours. I wondered if **she** called out to Christ for mercy in her final moments. I had a brief moment of panic that I would see her in heaven one day. But then I asked God to forgive my hard-heartedness.

To forgive my grudging forgiveness.

I prayed for her family. For the other children **she** had abused. I prayed that they would find the peace and salvation that I had been given in Jesus.

And I counted myself blessed.

I am so glad God is not like me. I am so glad that He did not hold a grudge against me for my sins against Him. I am so glad for Jesus. I am so glad for justice. I am so glad for mercy.

I am so glad that He pours His grace into my life every day.

LOOKING FORWARD WITH HOPE

Our world is filled with fear, hate, lust, greed, war, and utter despair. Surely the Second Coming of Jesus Christ is the only hope of replacing these depressing features with trust, love, universal peace, and prosperity.

(Billy Graham)

This book has been over 20 years in the writing. It has been incredibly painful as I have trawled the dusty corridors of childhood memories. Memories I thought I had long since locked away in secret vaults came out into the light as I began to tell my story.

Of course, my story is still being written. Only the Lord knows the ending.

But, I have a feeling that He isn't done with me yet.

I still have a lot of growing to do. But, thanks to Jesus, I see this world with new eyes. I see it through the lens of His pain and sacrifice, not my own.

I am not a victim anymore.

Of course, there are still so many unanswered questions. I still don't fully know why God allowed me to be abused. I know that I am not the only one. There are millions like us around the globe.

But, I do know that it isn't because God hates me, nor takes pleasure in my pain. On the contrary, He loves me. He loves you. He takes no pleasure in our suffering.

I take comfort in the knowledge that Jesus knows exactly how it feels because He has been in that position Himself. Never in a million years would we put our children through what happened to us. Yet, Jesus chose to enter into our experience, and much, much more, in order to rescue us. He came so that we could have peace with God. Yes He came to satisfy God's holy justice. But, He also came to bring a measure of healing to us. To offer us hope. To offer us some perspective on our pain. He wants us to know that everything we've been through is not in vain. That some gospel good can come out of the wreckage of our broken lives.

However, we won't find this peace, this healing and this hope *until* we come to Him in faith. Until we look at ourselves honestly, accept our own sins and recognise our need of Jesus as our Saviour.

That ache you feel in your heart right now is connected to the pain in your soul. God wants to ease that pain in your heart by saving your soul from an eternal torment that makes our past and present sufferings fade into insignificance.

Then, and only then, can we begin to come to terms with what has happened to us. Then, and only then, can we begin to move on. For some of us it will be a long road. It won't all be a bed of roses. We may find out things about ourselves that we don't like or find difficult to accept.

But, if we start by trusting in the Word of God, we can begin to heal. We can stop blaming ourselves. We can stop destroying ourselves. We can stop believing the lies about ourselves. We are not worthless. We are loved. We do mean something.

We can begin to move forward in life by dying *to* ourselves and living *for* Jesus.

By not looking back, but looking forward.

God will give us a new heart. A clean heart. A heart that searches after Him and not after vengeance. He will take away our nightmares and give us Jesus-centred dreams. He will give us new emotions – foreign emotions. We will learn to love again, or maybe for the first time. We will learn to trust again.

We will have a new spirit. God's Spirit. And He will stick with us right into eternity where we will live with our heavenly Father. There we will have a safe home. A home without pain. A home without shouting. A home where nobody is abused. A home where nobody sheds tears. A home where death no longer reigns.

A home filled with love, safety, peace and joy. The way it used to be. The way it should have been.

The way it will one day be again.

HELPFUL RESOURCES

WORSHIPPING WITH THE ENEMY? –INTERVIEW WITH A CHILD ABUSER

TELL ME ABOUT THE CRIMES YOU COMMITTED.

I molested two young boys, aged four & seven, over a year-long period of time. The eldest was my adopted son and the youngest was his cousin.

HOW WERE YOUR CRIMES DISCOVERED?

I turned myself in to the authorities. My conscience began to trouble me as I came to a realisation that what I was doing was wrong.

WHAT PUNISHMENT DID YOU RECEIVE?

I received a 50-year prison sentence and was released on probation after serving 11 years.

TELL ME HOW YOU CAME TO FAITH IN JESUS.

I was five years into my jail sentence and another convict started witnessing to me about the Lord. We became good friends and he began to study the Bible with me. Not long after that I gave my life to Christ.

Within weeks I was moved to another part of the prison and discovered some theology books by a man called R. C. Sproul.

They had been donated to the prison library and I read pretty much all of them.

HOW LONG HAVE YOU BEEN A CHRISTIAN?

I have been a Christian for almost eight years. I was released three years ago and discovered my current church a year after that.

WHY DID YOU WAIT A YEAR BEFORE GOING TO CHURCH?

I tried really hard to go to church but every church I contacted refused to let me worship with them because of the nature of my convictions.

Then, a mutual friend knew the pastor of my current church and contacted him to explain about my situation. We met at a coffee shop, I explained my background and testimony, and we went from there.

DID THIS PASTOR INFORM THE MEMBERS OF HIS CHURCH BEFORE ALLOWING YOU TO ATTEND?

All the members were made aware of my background prior to my arrival. There was no opposition to my attending, at least not to my knowledge.

WHAT ROLE DO YOU PLAY IN YOUR LOCAL CHURCH?

I am a member. I am very active socially. I'm also the church handyman.

WHAT WAS THE BIGGEST OBSTACLE IN YOUR COMING TO FAITH?

Forgiveness. The idea that God could forgive an offender like me. Not only that, He offers me ongoing forgiveness given my continual struggles with sin.

DO YOU HAVE A FAMILY OF YOUR OWN? DO THEY KNOW?

I am currently single. I lost custody of the children that were in my care. I am not allowed contact with them anymore.

DO YOU THINK YOU CAN YOU TRUST YOURSELF AROUND CHILDREN?

Yes and no. I keep myself accountable. I am close to several families. People always know where I am and what I am doing.

DO YOU DESERVE TO BE TRUSTED?

Not right now, no.

WHEN YOU HEAR STORIES OF TERRIBLE CHILD ABUSE, HOW DOES THAT MAKE YOU FEEL?

Sickened. It makes me regret that I am in that same category.

IF SOMEBODY ABUSED ONE OF YOUR LOVED ONES, HOW WOULD YOU FEEL?

Pretty upset. I would be angry if something happened to my little girl (he had a little girl who was never abused).

DO YOU STILL GET TEMPTED BY THOUGHTS OF SEXUAL DESIRE WITH BOYS?

Occasionally.

DO YOU STILL GET TEMPTED BY THOUGHTS OF YOUR PAST?

No.

WHAT DO YOU THINK MADE YOU DO THESE TERRIBLE THINGS?

I don't know. I was abused as a child for about a year between the ages of five and six. I sexually abused a minor for the first time at the age of 19 and I was 21 when I started doing it to the children in my care. I've always been attracted to young boys and noticed it first when I was 11.

I also had incorrect emotional connections and ideas of sex. I have an attraction to women, men, and boys, but not young girls. So these sexual urges pushed me further and further until it came to abusing children.

WHERE DID THESE 'INCORRECT CONNECTIONS' COME FROM?

From such an early age almost everything in my life was sexual.

HOW HAS YOUR LIFE CHANGED SINCE COMMITTING TO CHRIST? YOUR THOUGHTS AND DESIRES?

I still struggle with perversion. Before Christ I was bi-sexual (with consenting adults). That became normal and so I wanted to see how far I could take sexual pleasure by moving on to children.

My thought life now has changed dramatically. I see it as wrong, evil and an offence against not only against God but God's image bearers too.

Now I want to maintain sexual purity and operate within God's boundaries for what is acceptable.

DO YOU SEE YOURSELF STARTING A FAMILY IN THE FUTURE?

I have been heavily contemplating this. I want to be married and I am attracted to women. The question is, can I trust myself? What if we had sons? Would that be an issue? That weighs heavy on me.

WHAT MECHANISM IS IN PLACE SHOULD YOU FACE SERIOUS TEMPTATION IN YOUR LOCAL CHURCH FAMILY?

I have two people that I reach out to. They are my regular safeguards. The conditions of my probation mean that I must have a safety contract for being around minors. The pastor and I signed a contract detailing the rules and regulations for being part of the church. So, for instance, I have chaperones who accompany me in church. Also, I cannot be alone with a minor. I never use the public toilets in the church and have to use a private bathroom set aside for me.

HAVE YOU EVER BEEN IN CONTACT WITH ANY OF YOUR VICTIMS POST-CHRIST?
No.

HAVE YOU SOUGHT FORGIVENESS FROM ANY OF YOUR VICTIMS?
No. But that's down to the law, not my willingness. I am unable to have any contact with them.

HAVE YOU EVER HAD A NEGATIVE RESPONSE FROM A FELLOW CHRISTIAN?
Yes. Congregations have blacklisted me.

HOW DID ABUSING CHILDREN MAKE YOU FEEL?
It made me feel sexually gratified, and pleasured at the time. Even the pre-abuse was exhilarating. The post-abuse was filled with many feelings of guilt and lots of justifications. I had a lot of mixed emotions.

WHAT WERE SOME OF THE JUSTIFICATIONS?
During the abuse, I convinced myself that I wasn't an abuser. I told myself that what I was doing wasn't as serious as other people. I would often research child abusers online to figure out if I fit into that same category. But I couldn't admit that to myself. I told myself that the children enjoyed it and so that made it OK. I convinced myself that they weren't being harmed physically.

DID YOU EVER FEEL REMORSE?

Yes.

WHAT DID YOU DO WITH THAT REMORSE? HOW DID YOU DEAL WITH IT?

Initially I didn't deal with it and I don't know if I have fully dealt with it now. I am trying to be open and honest about the situation so people can see that I am changing and trying to change.

HOW WOULD YOU FEEL IF ONE OF YOUR ABUSE VICTIMS JOINED YOUR CHURCH?

Happy that God may have granted them salvation. Very confused. Scared.

HOW DO YOU FEEL ABOUT FORGIVENESS AND RECONCILIATION?

I don't expect to be forgiven by my victims. I would like to live my life honestly without re-offending and to help protect other children from abuse through education. Most people have keeping their kids safe all wrong.

CAN YOU UNPACK THAT LAST SENTENCE?

In child protection education there is a real push towards things like 'stranger danger' and 'good touch bad touch' teaching techniques. Yet, 95% of all victims are abused by a relative or a close friend of the family. That means if a father or mother figure touches them, then children aren't aware that they are being violated.

I think we should teach a child exclusively that it's their body and their private parts. There is no such thing as good touch bad touch. It is all bad touch (excluding medical professionals).

WHAT ADVICE DO YOU HAVE FOR CHURCHES?

Make sure you keep the idea of a child's private parts being private and make sure they know that any touch is inappropriate.

WHAT'S THE HARDEST THING ABOUT KNOWING WHAT YOU DID AND FOLLOWING JESUS?

Can I really be forgiven? And if God grants new life, why is there such a struggle with perversion still?

IN WHAT WAYS DO YOU STRUGGLE AND HOW DO YOU MORTIFY THE FLESH?

I get out of the house. Being alone makes the problem worse. I like staying busy. Reading Christian books. I get a daily morning text from my accountability men. I have limited internet access.

DO YOU WORRY ABOUT REOFFENDING?

Yes and no. As long as I stay regulated and aware of personal issues, I do very well. Accountability is the key for me. If I were given free rein and allowed to go about without guardrails I would put myself at serious risk of re-offending.

HOW CAN FELLOW CHRISTIANS BEST PRAY FOR YOU?

For my sanctification. Especially for my unnatural desires to go away. Pray that I would experience normalcy in relationships.

ANY FINAL COMMENTS?

There is no help for paedophiles. There are just accusations, so it is hard to come forward. If I were an alcoholic or a drug addict I would get help but in my case I can't.

INTERVIEW WITH THE PASTOR OF A CHILD ABUSER

WHEN DID YOU FIND OUT ABOUT HIS OFFENDING?

I knew because I had received an email from a local pastor who was looking for a church to place him in. The pastor had taken him into his church, but the congregation were unwilling to have him.

WHAT WAS YOUR INITIAL REACTION?

My initial reaction was to meet him in a coffee shop. We met and I listened to his story and the nature of his offences. He was under probation and had some legal obligations to keep. So, he has to have a certain number of chaperones who know about his crimes. In our church, we have a dozen men who have signed up to this (they sign a contract).

HOW DID THE CHURCH RESPOND?

Very well. Only the chaperones knew about his offending for the first few weeks. When we established that he would stay around, we went before the membership. We informed them of the precautions we were taking.

We explained to the members that because of the nature of his offences, he was forced to be up front about his sins. They, on the other hand, did not have to tell each other their secret sins and so he was being vulnerable to them. The members voted unanimously to accept him into the church and the fellowship has gone out of the way to be hospitable to him.

ARE THERE ANY PLACES OR MINISTRIES OFF LIMITS TO HIM?

He's not going to be working with children at all. He's also not eligible to do some ministries because of his crimes. We work in the local prison, a youth detention centre and an old person's home. They are out of bounds to him. However, he has done a lot of good work for a lot of members in terms of contracting and construction.

WHAT ADVICE WOULD YOU HAVE FOR OTHER CHURCHES AND LEADERS THINKING ABOUT ACCEPTING A CHILD ABUSER INTO THEIR FELLOWSHIP?

It is important for all the members of the church to know about the past offences. It's extremely important for a number of men to know about it, so that you can offer ongoing structure, accountability and discipleship.

HOW DO YOU KEEP HIM ACCOUNTABLE?

Chaperones. Somebody always has him within eyesight while he is on campus. We see all of his website visits on his iPad. We talk about his attractions at work (he is a building contractor) and how to avoid temptation and sin. In the church building he has his own private toilet and he is observed going in and out of it.

DO YOU TRUST HIM?

No, not fully. I trust him at some level because he is honest about his struggles. I have allowed him to do work at my house (alongside me) and I am aware of the strength of his temptations.

IF A NEW FAMILY COMES TO THE CHURCH DO YOU MAKE THEM AWARE OF HIS PRESENCE?

If they become members then we advise them.

DOES HE REQUIRE MORE, OR SPECIFIC KINDS OF, PASTORING THAT OTHER MEMBERS DON'T?

He doesn't require more from me. He does require it from more people in the congregation. There has to be a different kind of intentionality with him. For example, some people I don't worry about showing up early and leaving late. If it's him then he needs to be watched.

Not only are we trying to protect the children, but we are also looking out for him. We don't want him to be the subject of a false claim. We want to keep him from abusing children and dragging the name of Jesus into the mud.

DO YOU HAVE PEOPLE IN YOUR CHURCH WHO HAVE BEEN ABUSED IN THEIR CHILDHOOD OR IN OTHER RELATIONSHIPS?

Yes. Because they are believers and understand the nature of forgiveness, they don't seem to hold him responsible for what happened to them.

FAQS FROM CHILD ABUSE SUFFERERS

The following interview records the thoughts of three pastors, myself included, on some of the most frequent questions we have received on this subject. We have maintained the anonymity of Pastor A in order to protect the identity of the Christian in his church who has been convicted of child abuse offences.

Matthew is Matthew Spandler-Davison, a pastor from Kentucky and also the co-director of 20schemes, our church-planting ministry in Scotland.

HOW DO I GET RID OF THE FEELINGS THAT REMAIN AFTER SEXUAL ABUSE? HOW DO I AVOID FEELINGS OF PANIC AND VIOLATION AFTER I AM MARRIED?

PASTOR A: Some of that will have to be dealt with along with the spouse or soon-to-be spouse. There needs to be honest conversations and both parties will need patience and understanding. It will require significant effort to realise that the things that were done to them don't please God, but neither do they have to be defined by them. They need to be encouraged to see that abuse is not part of their identity in Jesus anymore. Also, we need to help them to see that marriage is nothing like what happened previously. What happened was a perversion of the good thing God has given for His people to enjoy. Under Jesus they can find healing and enjoy that which God gave for our pleasure.

MEZ: I would agree that those who have been victims need to pursue any and all relationships with openness and wisdom. Do not get married without telling your spouse of your history. Otherwise, when and if issues come up, it will prove difficult, although not impossible, to move forward together as a couple. Communication is so key to this. If sexual contact makes you feel panicked, then we need to make sure that the spouse understands this. We want to avoid cases of frustration and anger on the part of the non-abused spouse, which can be misinterpreted by abuse sufferers.

MATTHEW: Sometimes these feelings may take you by surprise. This was certainly the case for me. It was many years after the abuse and after I had married that such feelings of discomfort, disgust, and even panic surrounding sex and intimacy arose. The worst thing you can do at that point is to suppress those feelings. Bring them into the light. God has provided you with a spouse so that you might experience true intimacy, and that intimacy is more than just physical. It is also a place where you can be truly open about your past without fear. But don't stop there. You and your spouse might need to talk about it with a trained biblical counsellor. A counsellor can help you put your thoughts into words as you process some very painful emotions and memories.

HOW DO YOU FORGIVE A PERPETRATOR WHEN THERE IS NO REPENTANCE ON THEIR PART?

PASTOR A: I think it's a different type of forgiveness. Repentance is, primarily, between man and God. In one sense forgiving a perpetrator can sometimes lead to repentance. The abuser can be amazed as to why someone would forgive them, and that in turn could lead them to Christ.

I think we can forgive people in our heart after we have exhausted reasonable measures to contact the person (if legally allowable). You can write to them and let them know about the gospel that's saved you and the grace you've received. But these are things I would only counsel if you feel a strong conviction about it.

MEZ: This is a really tough one. As I said in the book, I never met with my chief abuser and, to be honest, I cannot remember the names and places of the other people. I never felt any real conviction to contact her over the years either. One of her children (my stepsister) did contact me through social media a couple of years ago. She, too, had moved away from her mother and was no longer in contact with her. We didn't stay in touch. It just brought back too many painful memories. As for myself, I just resolved in my heart not to engage in bitter thoughts about her when she, infrequently, popped into my mind. I decided that I wouldn't give room to any more poison within my soul and so just deliberately pushed it aside and left her to the Lord.

MATTHEW: As Mez has said, forgiveness doesn't always require you reaching out to the perpetrator of the abuse. One of my abusers died long before I ever told anyone about the abuse. I do not even know the name of the other. As a Christian the Holy Spirit has given me an unusual ability to not look back at those events or people with any sense of bitterness or anger – ask God to help you overcome that bitterness. So the first step is to resolve in your own heart to fight against feelings of hate or the desire for vengeance. Anger and bitterness can quickly become toxic in your own life and harm your other relationships. Please understand, though, the need to forgive does not mean you do not have the right to pursue justice. Forgiveness is not the absence of consequences or the removal of boundaries. If you still know your abuser, perhaps even still have a relationship with them, you should never feel guilty about bringing their abuse to light and putting in place measures to protect you from that person.

HOW SHOULD CHRISTIANS GO ABOUT FORGIVING CHILD ABUSERS?

PASTOR A: As horrific as it is, it is not the unpardonable sin. If God can forgive a child abuser – and He can – then we, as Christians, should have the capacity to also forgive them. The problem is that we often confuse forgiveness. It doesn't mean that we become gullible. We keep our heads up, our wits about us and exercise discernment in our forgiveness as we welcome them into the family of God.

MEZ: As a pastor I know what the correct answer is here. As a sufferer it has been far harder. Even when I have met child abusers in my ministry I have felt the tightness in my chest and the anger bubble up within me. Obviously, I have kept a deadpan expression. I am 20 years into my faith now and so it is far easier for me to be calmer and more considered about things. I accept that God does save child abusers. He saves murderers. He saves rapists. They don't deserve His grace, but then again, neither do I. That's what I tell myself and that's what I intentionally remind myself when emotions sometimes threaten to overspill.

MATTHEW: In many ways, this is the scandal of grace. How could God forgive someone who has wilfully permitted such an ugly offence against a child? Yet, we know that the love of Christ is sufficient to overcome all sins – no matter how repulsive we might find them. This is the very essence of the gospel. If we say that anyone is out of the reach of God's grace, mercy and forgiveness, then how could any one of us have any certainty that we are forgiven? So, we too must find within us the love of God that enables us to demonstrate love and forgiveness to even the vilest of sinners who has turned from their sin and put their trust in Jesus as their Lord.

WHAT WISDOM AND TRUTH SHOULD WE CLING ONTO WHEN DEALING WITH A SEX OFFENDER?

PASTOR A: The gospel is powerful enough in God's hands to save them. At the same time they still battle the old man and he will be putting up a strong fight. We cannot ignore that. Converted abusers feel very confident in the early days that they won't do it again (like most new Christians). They let their guards down and, if not careful, so can the church. This can lead to falling back into that sin. We all have sins we go back to in moments of stress. We all must be constantly vigilant in our fight against sin.

MEZ: I wrote a book called *War: Why Did Life Just Get Harder?*[1] From the moment of conversion until the moment of death we are all in a spiritual war. We are justified upon conversion, but we are subject to attacks from the flesh, the devil and the world as we wait to go to glory. It is a fact that we all tend to have 'go to' sins when we come under pressure and feel temptation to sin. We have to teach child abusers that they must be ever vigilant

---

1   *War: Why Did Life Just Get Harder?* (Ross-Shire: Chirstian Focus Publications, 2017).

in their war against their sinful desires and perverted lusts. We also have to tell them that they cannot trust themselves. If they could, then they wouldn't have found themselves in their current situation.

Also, people who commit these kinds of offences are master liars and manipulators. So, I would engage with them and listen to what they say with a great deal of discernment. Don't take anything at face value. Often people will confess things to me to mask other, more serious sins going on in the background which they want to keep secret.

MATTHEW: Let me speak specifically here to church leaders as it relates to ministering to a sex offender. In my own church we had a sex offender attend our services for some time and it caused us to think hard about this subject. First, be sure to run criminal background checks on all your workers engaged in any activity with minors. This should be standard practice for every church. Second, have a robust child protection policy and provide training for your members. Third, consider a Church Safety Plan that sets out protocols for how you will respond when you become aware of an accusation of child abuse (or abuse of any kind) and ensure that you involve the relevant authorities immediately if there is any accusation of illegal activity. Fourth, and this relates to the question, if you become aware of a registered sex offender attending your services you have a duty to both protect the church and to minister to the offender. Communicate to the church both the identity of the offender and the plan in place to safeguard the church and minister to the offender. Designate a person to act as his escort so that he is never in the building unmonitored. Ensure there is a person providing ongoing accountability and discipleship to the offender and establish a way for that person to regularly report to the elders. Provide meaningful ways that the offender can serve and find a sense of place and purpose in the life of the church without it involving contact with minors.

HOW HARD IS IT TO FORGIVE?

PASTOR A: It's impossible with man. But not with God. The Christian who has been made new, and understands the nature of the gospel and the fallen world, should be the best at forgiving.

MEZ: Forgiveness is a supernatural act. I truly believe we can only really, deeply forgive people from the heart after God has done a work in us through the power of His Holy Spirit. Even then I think the process of coming around to full forgiveness can take many years for people.

MATTHEW: There is a difference between forgiveness and restoration. Forgiveness can take time, so don't feel guilty if you are reading this and you are just not there yet. Ask God to give you the desire to forgive because you have a desire to show God that you love and trust Him. That is where it starts. Restoration is an altogether different issue. You cannot restore someone who does not recognise the hurt they have caused and who is not willing to do all that they can to turn away from it and make amends for it. So, you can forgive someone in your own heart and mind without having to pursue an ongoing relationship with that person.

HOW CAN WE COUNSEL VICTIMS TO TRUST AGAIN IN FUTURE RELATIONSHIPS?

PASTOR A: Help them to trust God and then a couple of trustworthy people God has brought into their life. Make sure that relationships are a slow, methodical process. God is trustworthy. Also, people fail us. God will not.

MEZ: Trust is perhaps almost as difficult as forgiveness for survivors. I know that I went into every relationship expecting it to fail, or to be let down, for years after my abuse stopped. I was the life and soul of the party and had lots of friends, but I didn't trust a person enough to tell them any of my secrets or what had happened to me. Only after I came to faith and met my now-wife did trust build up. I am still quite guarded in my friendships but I do have several close friends whom I would trust with my life.

MATTHEW: I recently realised that even years after my abuse it was still affecting the relationships I have today. I know hundreds of people but I rarely let anyone get close to me. I found ministry to be a great place to hide. I could just deal with other people's problems and ignore my own. The truth is, though, we need friends, and we need people in our life whom we can trust and rely on. God has created opportunities for us to be able to trust and to be able to get close to others. God has established His people into a community which He calls the church. A true, healthy church is a community of men and women who love and trust and care well for one another. God created marriage as a safe place where we can be vulnerable and truly open and unashamed. It is okay to be guarded but it is rarely helpful to be closed off and shut down. Over time we learn to trust, and when we do we experience intimacy, this is most noticeable in our personal relationship with God.

CAN WE BOTH FORGIVE OUR ABUSER AND HOPE FOR THEM TO BE PUNISHED AT THE SAME TIME?

PASTOR A: Absolutely. In fact I think we ought to. Christians fail too often in pursuing righteousness and justice. The law demands that offences are punished. Punishment often leads to a change of heart and a change of life. Therefore, real love demands that justice be pursued. It also protects others because it's very rare for perpetrators to have only one victim.

MEZ: I hope so. That's how I felt for many years. My issue would be to ensure that a person was pursuing justice and not vengeance. Vengeance belongs to the Lord. But I have great respect for those who pursue their abusers and see them brought to justice. I sometimes still wonder if I should have pursued justice in my case.

MATTHEW: Yes. The old adage 'forgive and forget' is nonsense. Forgiveness does not remove the consequences. An abuser who acknowledges the pain they have caused and who seeks the forgiveness of those who they have hurt will not run away from the consequences of their actions. But be sure we are pursuing justice and not pursuing hurt and pain and misery to come the way of the perpetrator. We need to do a gut check to see what is driving our desire for the person to be punished. Is it a pursuit of justice or a desire that they suffer?

WHAT WOULD BE YOUR ADVICE TO THOSE OF US WHO MINISTER IN SCHEME/COUNCIL ESTATE CONTEXTS, WHERE AN ABUSER'S LIFE WOULD BE AT RISK WITHIN THE COMMUNITY OUTSIDE THE CHURCH?

PASTOR A: It's tough because my view on regeneration says there is a place in the kingdom for all types of sinners. Maybe helping them move to a different scheme and place where the church leaders are fully aware. It's difficult when you are ministering to first-generation Christians who have been abused.

MEZ: This is where it gets difficult. I work in a closed community. My church is in the centre of that community and we are well known and established there. A church that operates as a gathering – in other words, where people come from a wide geographical spread – can afford to take more risks with welcoming offenders into the church family. In my community, their life would almost certainly be in danger from local residents. Many of my abused members would also be fearful for their safety. Finally, our witness would be compromised if we were known to shelter abusers.

None of these are good enough reasons, on their own, to refuse help to an abuser, but I would be very, very hesitant in knowingly accepting one into membership of the church. Having said this, that would be my personal view and would not necessarily reflect the view of our eldership and a majority of our membership.

At the very least, I would counsel extreme caution and would perhaps want to see if we could help them get into another church where they wouldn't face the same dangers and issues they would face in our community.

MATTHEW: In a tight-knit community it is impossible to hide. Our sin and our shame follow us. A sex offender is especially at risk of being outed and targeted by vigilante behaviour. Where possible, a reformed and repentant offender needs to be able to worship at a place away from any victims of their abuse. The way we help them is by helping them move and find a church in another community.

HOW CAN CHRISTIANS PRAY FOR BOTH THE ABUSED AND THE ABUSERS IN OUR CHURCHES?

PASTOR A: Christians should pray for the abused and the abuser because both are in situations of immense need and only God has what each of them need. The abused needs mercy from God so that their identity is not in being abused but in God who made them in His own image. For the abuser, pray for God to save them so that their soul might be saved from Hell while also trusting Him to display His righteousness and justice here on earth.

MATTHEW:

PRAYING FOR THE ABUSED

When you are with someone who has shared that they have suffered from abuse in their childhood then offer to pray with them then and there. Take seriously their pain and their sense of vulnerability. Don't presume that you understand what they are experiencing. Pray with them so they might grow in confidence that they can take their hurts and their pains to a God who loves them and has compassion for them.

Pray regularly for those who have shared with you about abuse. Often times from the moment they share they will start to become aware of memories, reliving past pains and hurts, and be overcome with guilt and shame. So, pray often for them, that they will be strong and at peace. May your prayers for them prompt you to regularly check in on them so they do not shut down or be overcome by feelings of unworthiness or even guilt for sharing with you.

PRAYING FOR THE ABUSER

For a believer who has confessed to a history of committing abuse, they need to have the courage to walk in faith and repentance even though the human consequences for their behaviour will be devastating. As you pray with them you are signalling that although they have acted in a shocking manner they are not separated from the love of God if they truly walk in faith and repentance. They will be tempted to run, to hide, or even to fall into despair. They need to hear the power of the gospel that can overcome the most shocking of sins. They need to daily lean on Christ to go to war against the flesh. Pray with them to point them to Christ who is their redeemer and saviour.

MEZ: We need to pray that both would come to an understanding of the sin in their life, and their need to turn from that, and confess Jesus as Lord. If I'm being brutally honest, I would have an easier time praying for the abused rather than the abuser.

Pray that the victim would not remain crippled by a victim mentality but receive grace, mercy and forgiveness in Jesus. Not only that. But that they, over time would come to a place of love, mercy and forgiveness toward their abuser(s). Pray that they would find the freedom that comes from handing their pain over to Jesus. Pray that they would trust the Lord of all the earth to one day dispense His ultimate justice.

As for abusers, we should pray that they would not be in denial of their grievous sin. That they would face up to, and own, the perversions of their behaviour. Pray that they would find healing and forgiveness, likewise, in the gospel of Jesus. As Christians we ought to pray that our hearts would soften toward these kinds of people, as we realise that we all stand justly condemned before a holy and righteous God. Finally, pray that they would lean into Jesus and rely on His Holy Spirit as they face the trials and temptations particular to their spiritual battles.

A RESPONSE TO THIS BOOK FROM AN ABUSE SUFFERER

HOW LONG HAVE YOU BEEN A CHRISTIAN?

I have been a Christian for seven years.

HOW AWARE ARE YOUR CHURCH FAMILY ABOUT YOUR HISTORY?

There's a very select few, maybe four or five, that know a short, vague version. I don't really talk about it. But, I know that in order to heal and move on, I need to talk about it with some people. I need to help people become aware of my triggers and to help me to process my emotions.

I have been more open with my accountability partner/mentor and have asked to discuss things I would normally avoid. She's very patient (it's taken us five years to get to this point). I wish I could be more open, but I'm fearful and have a hard time trusting people. That is changing as I begin to trust more and more.

HOW DO YOU FEEL ABOUT YOUR ABUSER(S)?

I've done a good job of pretending he doesn't exist, but every day at some point, a memory pops into my head. I feel hate, betrayed, angry, repulsed, sick to my stomach, and I feel let down and damaged – he caused that. I feel that he deserves hell because he made me feel like I was living hell. He has never admitted to what he has done to me and others, he has never taken responsibility for wrecking people's lives. I have seen him once since my family were able to escape and the feeling of fear is still there. He is currently serving a prison sentence, but I fear one day he will be released and I will be confronted by the past again. I can't get my head around why someone could treat another human being like that, as if they were nothing and disposable.

WHAT DID YOU THINK ABOUT THE BOOK?

The book is needed. There's lots of practical help in there and steps for everyone, for the abused, the abuser or the person walking alongside. It wasn't just a textbook throwing out Bible verses, but real stories. It wasn't all fluffy and nice, but a reminder that God hates evil. It helped me to see how our suffering isn't without reason and in some way good can be brought out of it.

This is something I have struggled with for a long time. *'What possible good can come from a situation like that?'* But I look at my life now and it's good, despite my struggles to process my past. I get to share the life-changing news of Jesus Christ every day. I have a wonderful church family that have modelled family to me, who have loved me well and who challenge me.

I have a sympathy for people that can only come from experiencing the things they have felt.

WHAT DID YOU NOT LIKE ABOUT THE BOOK?

The book brought my own sin to the surface and challenged me.

WHAT DID YOU STRUGGLE WITH MOST?

The challenge that my sin is no worse than anybody else's. Even writing that makes me feel uneasy. We know in this world there is a rank of sins, and anything to do with a child is at the top. But, actually the Bible says that sin is sin.

Also, my own view of judgment is very different to God's. I struggle with praying for God to help me forgive because I don't want to. I know I cannot do it on my own. I know I should forgive. I'm a Christian, but I feel if I forgive, they will have won. Also, my family, who are not Christians, would feel like I've betrayed them.

Also, if I forgive, will it mean my suffering didn't matter?

I'm at the stage of my Christian walk where I want to move on. I want to be used by God for His kingdom and not dwell on the pains of the path. This book will help to do that and I pray it helps others too.

WHAT DID YOU LEARN?

Just knowing God has a good purpose for our suffering. That God is angry toward those that abuse people, even more angry than me! But it's God who will have the final say. I can't keep the bitterness inside me, and have it eat me up inside. I can't let shame silence me. I can't allow what happened to me to poison every aspect of my life, including friendships and relationships. I have to accept that my responses don't affect my abuser one bit. They just end up hurting me and those I love.

God will bring final judgement. He already has in Jesus and so I trust that.

WHAT WAS MOST HELPFUL TO YOU?

It's easy for me to remain in a victim mentality mode. So, to have that challenged is good. I am responsible for my actions before God. I can't blame everything on the fact I was abused as a child.

HAVE YOU CHANGED YOUR MIND ABOUT ANYTHING AFTER READING THE BOOK?

The idea of a child abuser coming to faith was the most unrealistic thing I could ever imagine. Surely not? But, why not? Did I think the gospel wasn't powerful enough for that? No. More like I didn't believe God would do that to people. I feel by saving abusers, God is hitting me with one last sucker punch. Yet, the gospel is real and changing lives. It changed mine.

WHAT DID YOU THINK ABOUT THE INTERVIEW WITH THE CONVERTED CHILD ABUSER?

I didn't want to read it. I have anger towards the man and I don't even know him! But I think it's a good example of how God can change people's lives. Even those kinds of people! And, even though I don't understand it, God knows what He's doing. Forgiveness is for all people.

HOW HAS BECOMING A CHRISTIAN HELPED YOU TO DEAL WITH YOUR PAST?

I think I am still dealing with it. There's lots of healing still to be done, but I've healed more in the last seven years than I did in the thirteen before knowing Jesus. I may never understand my suffering, but I rest in the One who does. Jesus knows my suffering. He cares for and loves me far better than anyone who walks this earth.

I also recognise that I am a sinner and there's no excuse for my sin. In fact, it was my sin that put Jesus on the cross. The sin of each of us. Also, I have God's Word and prayer. That is a gift and privilege. Before trusting Jesus I found comfort in drinking and inflicting pain upon myself. Now, I'm trying every day to find comfort in God's promises. I read the Psalms often and I cry out to

God because I know He hears. He may answer differently to the way I think He should, but He's God, and I'm not.

HOW HAS THE LOCAL CHURCH HELPED YOU?

I'm learning to trust people again. My church family are a bunch of wretched sinners, who try to love each other well. They want to live for God's glory. They model family, which is something I've always craved. They invite me to be a part of their individual families and I feel loved and cared for by them.

Also, the men in my church have taught me what men should be like, and what it actually looks like to care for, and lead, your family. I'm thankful for them. They have helped me change my perception of men without even knowing it.

WHAT ADVICE WOULD YOU GIVE TO SOMEONE SUFFERING ABUSE AT HOME?

I'm sorry and my heart aches for you. I wish I had a magic wand to fix things, but I don't. I do want to walk this pain with you and introduce you to someone who is far more powerful than any predator out there: Jesus.

You may not feel like God loves you because of your suffering and, trust me, I know that feeling. Pre-Christ I felt so angry towards God. If He was really real and really loved me, then He wouldn't let me suffer like this. He does love us and we know this because of the work of Jesus.

Seek help. I know that is easier said than done. It might even feel impossible. But, find someone you trust and tell them. I feel that once something is out in the open, then there is a responsibility for others to help. It took me 20 years after my abuse to speak out for the first time.

No amount of drinking, staying away from relationships, pretending to be someone I wasn't, or self-harm brought me peace. Know that you are far more valuable and loved than your circumstances suggest. You are not your abuse and you are not to blame for your abuse.

There is help and people out there willing to listen. But, most importantly, God sees and hears. He hasn't abandoned you as you may think He has. It's only when we truly know Jesus that we will have peace. That doesn't mean it's plain sailing from here. It isn't. I battle every day. I have doubts. But the battle has been won. Jesus won it for us.

HOW DO YOU THINK YOU WOULD COPE IF A CHILD ABUSER CAME INTO MEMBERSHIP OF YOUR LOCAL CHURCH?

Truthfully, I'm not sure. I don't like the idea. Actually, it terrifies me a little. I would definitely feel scared. I would battle with feeling that they don't deserve to be in church and they don't deserve God's grace. But, ultimately, I would need to trust my elders to know what is best.

NEXT STEPS

We started out asking some tough questions. From the outset, I mentioned who I hoped might be reading this book...

It is for the Christian wondering if God truly does love them.

It is for the sceptic and the unbeliever who wonders if God exists and, if He does, why He would allow such things to happen.

It's for the perpetrators of such vile acts who wonder if their dark deeds will ever be discovered.

It's for the ones who turned their backs on their evil sins and found the cure of forgiveness and peace in Jesus.

And it's for those who are just not there yet; who wonder if they can ever forgive. Or if they can ever love. If they can ever rebuild their lives.

Well if that describes you, then now what?

No doubt reading this book has been as difficult for you as writing it has been for me. I am not interested in this being just another book. I don't want you to remain in the silence. For too long we have been silent sufferers with hidden wounds.

So, what should you do now?

STEP ONE

First, you have to start with yourself. You cannot undo your past and you cannot change what has happened. As much as we want to, we may not be able to understand why it happened, but we can change ourselves. We can change our own way of thinking and the path we are on.

Start by admitting that we are all sinners, that the whole human race has turned its back on their creator.

That we have all lived life according to our own rules. That we have denied or ignored God.

Submit to the truth that our only hope in this life and the next is found through faith in Jesus.

> There is only one light in this world.
> There is only one person who can save.
> There is no other.

We cannot be saved from the pain of the past. But we can be saved from the coming wrath. We can ensure that the torment we feel now does not live with us into eternity.

> We do that by running to Jesus.
> By reaching out to Him.
> By trusting in Him.

This life is not all there is for us. What has happened to you in your past does not need to define your future. This life is more than being born, being abused, suffering, dying and then being forgotten.

> There is forgiveness for us.
> There is acceptance for us.
> There is healing for us.

It is found in Jesus. Pick up the New Testament and meet Him there if you do not already know Him. Find a Christian and ask them to read it with you.

> There will be justice for all evildoers.
> The God of all the earth will do right.
> He will punish the guilty.
> Our pain matters because His pain made it so.

But we cannot live this life being torn apart by our own anger and bitterness and guilt and shame. We can find a place where that can be dealt with once and for all. To do that we too must repent – change our mind – towards God and walk in a new life with Jesus.

STEP TWO

You need to find a good local church. I don't just mean any church. There are loads out there that may not do you any good. The kind of church you need to look for is one where the Bible is preached, where the good news of Jesus is celebrated, and where the members truly know how to support and care well for one another. We call this kind of church a healthy church.

Why do you need to find a church? Because, like all of us, you need other Christians in your life who can pray for you, encourage you and give you wise counsel when things get tough (which they will). We can't keep doing this on our own. God has provided a place where we can be well cared for. A place where we can be open and honest with others. That is His church, His family, and we desperately need a place where we can belong, where we can grow and where we can serve.

If you don't know where to start then contact us. We will be very happy to find a church for you. Look me up on Twitter or reach out to us at 20schemes.com

STEP THREE

You might need to get some counselling. That is not a sign of weakness; it is actually a sign of strength. When I say counselling, I don't mean going to sit on a therapist's couch to just share all your innermost thoughts. I mean find someone who will help you to think with wisdom and maturity about what you have experienced. Find someone you can trust. A place where you can open up about your hurts and your struggles. Someone who will help you to navigate well how to overcome those nagging feelings of guilt and shame and bitterness and hate. We call this kind of counsellor a *biblical counsellor* because what they are doing is helping apply the truths of the Bible to some of the hurts we have experienced in this life. There are some great resources online to help you locate a counsellor like that (CCEF, biblicalcounselling.org, etc), or again you can reach out to us or speak to your pastor.

STEP FOUR

Pray. You need to pray now. You need God's help. I would suggest you start writing out your prayers. It may help you to work through those thoughts that are all muddled up in your head right now. A great place to start when praying is the Psalms. Read a psalm. Pray that psalm. Write down in a journal what God might be teaching you as you do it.

Celebrate. God is not done with you. There is much good that God is still going to do in your life. You are not defined by what you have done or what has been done to you. You are defined by what Jesus has done and all that He has done for you. There is much to celebrate. He loves you. He is with you. And if you cry out to Him, He will receive you.

Also available from Christian Focus Publications...

Eryl Davies

HIDDEN EVIL
A Biblical & Pastoral Response
To Domestic Abuse

Hidden Evil

A Biblical and Pastoral Response to Domestic Abuse

D. Eryl Davies

Domestic abuse is an ugly, but all too real, problem that is often not dealt with well within our churches. Eryl Davies tells the stories of domestic abuse survivors – both men and women – who have been let down by their churches' reactions. How are we to respond biblically to such situations? How do pastors and church leaders address this problem when both victim and abuser are part of their congregation? As well as making the reader aware of the reality of this issue, Davies gives helpful guidelines and suggestions for church leaders dealing with cases of domestic abuse.

... wakes us up to the disturbing reality that the church is not immune to the horrors of domestic abuse ... Yet this is not something the church knows how to handle. Davies gives us the data and tools we need to dig our heads out of the sand and help those in danger!

Natalie Brand
Lecturer, Union School of Theology, Bridgend, South Wales

978-1-5271-0331-3

NO MORE HURTING

LIFE BEYOND SEXUAL ABUSE
GWEN PURDIE

No More Hurting

Life Beyond Sexual Abuse

Gwen Purdie

To many of us sexual abuse is a bewildering and deeply uncomfortable topic. News reports on the issue are greeted with a shake of the head as we think of the damage done, however in most cases, as the news continues, our minds gratefully move on to more comfortable areas. What do we do when we are faced with someone who has suffered abuse? – Or if you yourself have suffered abuse?

This book is a thoroughly Christian response to issues surrounding sexual abuse and shouts that there is LIFE after abuse. It is a frank look at a complex situation that affects more people than we would want to believe. It shows how to deal with many of the symptoms that those who have been abused are likely to suffer.

When reading this book one realises that God not only cares deeply for the abused, but that He has spoken directly to them in the pages of the Bible.

Stephen McQuoid
General Director of Gospel Literature Outreach, Motherwell, Scotland

978-1-8579-2679-8

GOD

IS HE OUT THERE?

MEZ MCCONNELL

WAR

WHY DID LIFE JUST GET HARDER?

MEZ MCCONNELL

VOICES

WHO AM I LISTENING TO?

ANDY PRIME

BIBLE

CAN WE TRUST IT?

ANDREW MATHIESON

BELIEVE

WHAT SHOULD I KNOW?

MIKE MCKINLEY

First Steps Series

This series of short workbooks are designed to help you think through some of life's big questions.

1. GOD: Is He Out There?

2. WAR: Why Did Life Just Get Harder?

3. VOICES: Who Am I Listening To?

4. BIBLE: Can We Trust It?

5. BELIEVE: What Should I Know?

6. CHARACTER: How Do I Change?

7. TRAINING: How Do I Grow As A Christian?

8. CHURCH: Do I Have To Go?

9. RELATIONSHIPS: How Do I Make Things Right?

10. SERVICE: How Do I Give Back?

CHURCH IN HARD PLACES

An initiative of Acts 29

TRAIN   RESOURCE   EQUIP   INTEGRATE

APPRENTICESHIPS

A two year, fully funded non-residential training program designed to equip and assess leaders in the poorest communities around the globe.

WORKSHOPS

One day events designed to build momentum, relationships, and help local churches & leaders develop a robust vision for reaching the poor communities within the cities they live.

COACHING

Our coaching groups are a way for leaders already engaged in ministry to the urban poor to gain further insight, advice, networking, and encouragement from leaders working in similar contexts.

BECOME A SPONSOR!

Sign up to sponsor the training and development of one of our apprentices.

FOR MORE INFORMATION VISIT
churchinhardplaces.com

@churchinhardplaces on social media

Christian Focus Publications

Our mission statement —

STAYING FAITHFUL

In dependence upon God we seek to impact the world through literature faithful to His infallible Word, the Bible. Our aim is to ensure that the Lord Jesus Christ is presented as the only hope to obtain forgiveness of sin, live a useful life and look forward to heaven with Him.

Our books are published in four imprints:

CHRISTIAN
FOCUS

Popular works including biographies, commentaries, basic doctrine and Christian living.

CHRISTIAN
HERITAGE

Books representing some of the best material from the rich heritage of the church.

MENTOR

Books written at a level suitable for Bible College and seminary students, pastors, and other serious readers. The imprint includes commentaries, doctrinal studies, examination of current issues and church history.

CF4•K

Children's books for quality Bible teaching and for all age groups: Sunday school curriculum, puzzle and activity books; personal and family devotional titles, biographies and inspirational stories — because you are never too young to know Jesus!

Christian Focus Publications Ltd,
Geanies House, Fearn, Ross-shire,
IV20 1TW, Scotland, United Kingdom.
www.christianfocus.com